CARRY-ON BAGGAGE

HOWARD FELDMAN

Copyright © Howard Feldman with Batya Green-Bricker
Jerusalem 2015/5775

All rights reserved. No part of this publication may be translated, reproduced, stored in a retrieval system or transmitted, in any form or by any means, electronic, mechanical, photocopying, recording or otherwise, without express written permission from the publishers.

Cover Design: mr design

ISBN: 978-965-229-855-3

2 4 6 8 9 7 5 3 1

Gefen Publishing House Ltd.	Gefen Books
6 Hatzvi Street	11 Edison Place
Jerusalem 94386, Israel	Springfield, NJ 07081
972-2-538-0247	516-593-1234
orders@gefenpublishing.com	orders@gefenpublishing.com

www.gefenpublishing.com

Printed in Israel   *Send for our free catalog*

Library of Congress Control Number: 2015945257

To Heidi

My drop of normal in a sea of chaos

CONTENTS

Introduction vii
Chapter One: A World of Fiction 1
Chapter Two: Raising the Banner 6
Chapter Three: School Bags 12
Chapter Four: Holding The Banner When The
    South Easter Blows 26
Chapter Five: In Search of an Astounding Career 32
Chapter Six: Tampered Luggage 41
Chapter Seven: Packing and Unpacking 46
Chapter Eight: Pitching a Banner in Hebrew 52
Chapter Nine: Going Global 57
Chapter Ten: Life After Death 67
Chapter Eleven: Time Change 73
Chapter Twelve: Telephone Calls 87
Chapter Thirteen: The Magic of Metal 93
Chapter Fourteen: The Shadow with a Family 103
Chapter Fifteen: Blue, Blue, Blue, Blue, ~~Blue~~, Pink 110
Chapter Sixteen: Master of the Universe –
    Worshipping the Master of the Universe 121
Chapter Seventeen: Up To Speed 126
Chapter Eighteen: The Perfect Storm 129
Chapter Nineteen: Low Iron 132
Chapter Twenty: Broken Baggage 138
Chapter Twenty One: Toppling the Giant 142
Chapter Twenty Two: Where do you go to, My Lovely? 147
Chapter Twenty Three: Luggage for Carrying On 155
Acknowledgements 158

INTRODUCTION

I WAS LATE for a meeting with my lawyer. And I hate being late. Moving with purpose into my office, I grabbed my keys, cellphone, BlackBerry, wallet and sunglasses, walked briskly past my PA down the stairs towards my car that was parked outside the office building, and not in the parking I had assigned myself in the underground parking lot. My white Jaguar XKR glistened in the Johannesburg morning sun as I hastened towards it. The drive was a quick one, out of the prestigious Melrose Arch complex, to the right towards Corlett Drive where his chambers were. I had just enough time to call my in-house attorney in order to understand the salient points of the meeting ahead. It was also enough time for me to be followed and not enough time to notice. Five minutes later my life would change.

It took me a second to process the fact that I was being attacked. As he ran toward me I was overwhelmed by the sense that I was a participant in a movie that I hadn't seen. Yet I had to play the role of the victim, and followed a basic instinct that as long as I did not do anything to startle or alarm him, I would be ok. I had no sense as to what he wanted until he screamed at me to remove my watch, all whilst gesturing with the gun that was so close to my face I could see each indentation. I have no experience with guns, but this one will stay carved into my mind forever. I was on the phone with Liza, our legal counsel and as he ripped the phone from my hand, I felt the link to anyone outside snap, and I was very much alone. I had put my wallet inside the door panel and was about to reach to get it, but something stopped me as I realised he didn't ask for it and I would only give him what he demanded. That thought process might well have saved my life, as reaching your hand to where it cannot be seen could be viewed as threatening to a person with a gun and anything could have happened. I hardly saw the person attached to it. He was wearing a balaclava – dehumanising him – something that would torment me for many months, as I would never know if the person I was encountering was the one who attacked me. Indeed, maybe I would thank him as this event started a process in my life that I am deeply grateful for.

But at the time and for the weeks after it I couldn't see that.

He took my Limited Edition Rose Gold Panerai, approximate value EU28,000 – the favourite in my collection and that made me mad, really mad.

An hour later I was back at work.

A month later I got sick.

Three months later it happened again.

I was followed home. This time there were three of them. They had shotguns and they were angry. They didn't care that I had a security guard at my home, they didn't care that they were being filmed. Like the quintessential 21st century nightmare, I have it on tape where I am free to watch my repeated humiliation over and over and over ... it is noteworthy that when I think of the scene, what stays with me most is not the perpetrators running towards me, their aggression, the shotguns, or my fear, but watching myself climb out of my car put my hands on my head in submission, in disbelief, and indeed in sorrow. This time they took my watch (also a Panerai), my wallet with my driver's license and credit cards, my cellphone and my BlackBerry, my passport, my computer and personal papers, as well as my new Tumi carry-on that I had purchased for the trip. They also took with them my faith in the world that I had created.

An hour later I was not back at work.

A month later I went back to the office.

Three months later I shut my business down.

I could no longer carry the banner.

Chapter One

A WORLD OF FICTION

THE WORLD I had constructed was a marvellous one. It was a place where nice guys could finish first, even in the cut-throat aggressive world of commodity trading. It was a world where suppliers and customers were genuine friends, and it was accepted that everyone had the right to make a buck. It was a place where you knew that as a business you contributed to supply-chain efficiencies and where you had real relationships with competitors. In my world, anyone could share a drink and a laugh. It was a world of lovable rogues, of hard-nosed businessmen-with-heart, and where secretly and modestly, everyone was doing as much good as possible. Business travel was done in style and 1A was your seat of choice. Hotel check-in was never at the general reception and washing was returned on the same day. Families were supportive and intact, and no one really suffered from the mental and physical absence of dad. It was a place where beggars knew your name and chatted happily at traffic lights, and where others were proud of your success.

This was my carefully crafted world, but it was not real. Yet it was, for a time, a seemingly happy place. It was held together by a thread of positive and by a staple of denial. But with two traumatic events and a poor trading year, it came apart at the seams.

When exposed, and looking through decidedly untinted glasses, I now saw a colourless world that I had pretended didn't exist. Suddenly everyone was in it for themselves, no one really wanted to do business with you. And no one was secretly philanthropic. Beggars smirked with aggression as they lurched towards your car. If they knew your name and you theirs, it was only to extort you further. The planes were ageing and the hotels were soiled. It was grey and it was dark and there was very little joy.

I was tired. I could no longer delude myself that the world was indeed the one I had devised.

Contemporary thought extols the virtues of promoting yourself as a brand. Ironically, the brand that I created for myself was "honesty". I fought the causes of the underdog in a positive and constructive way. I took the high road when faced with conflict and "said what I feel" in a way that would make people hear me, and not feel threatened. I became a master of presentation and could sell anything to anyone.

I was a business and community leader and a donor. I had built a company with six offices around the world, the largest trader of Chrome Ore globally, I was charitable, Chairman of the South African Jewish Report, had donated buildings and was on most donors lists. I was taken seriously. There was a lot to be proud of. I didn't gamble. I didn't drink excessively. My marriage was strong, my kids were connected to me and I had real relationships with them. Our home, a magnificent structure, was a warm and welcoming place that saw quite literally hundreds of people, of all ages visiting over the weekend. The kitchen churned out cakes and delicacies, good coffees, single malt whiskeys and good wines (but not in excess of course). The sun always seemed to shine on the beautiful garden and manicured lawns. Our home had become like a community centre where teenagers could gather in safe, but appropriately cool surroundings, and where parents knew that their offspring were cared for. The key to our front door was on the outside door and our home was a place of refuge. Weddings, even those of strangers, were commonplace in our garden and people shook their heads in wonderment. Our goals were lofty and we developed the notion that our responsibility was to do as much good as possible and save the world – one person and one cause at a time.

And we did, or at least we tried. We never said no, or at least we tried not to. We supported as many charities as we could manage, even if the cause was not one that really resonated. I did volunteer work for the Jewish Burial Society and Heidi volunteered at the Old Age Home. She baked and cooked and delivered home-made meals to anyone in need and we shrugged off disappointment in others with the confidence that only the self-righteous can feel. We hosted and we supported and we got involved. We counselled and advised and we guided. We were not spectators, but central to the game of life. The deal that we made with ourselves when buying our house is that we would use it for as much "greater good" as was possible, and so would host everything from meetings to lectures to breakfasts to weddings and we didn't appear to tire. We would not say no to those requesting any assistance and we did so with genuine care.

To say that this banner was all unreal, or negative, would be untrue. The banner exposed my family and me to things of lasting value. We were also the hosts for many international visitors who would come to Johannesburg. We welcomed them into our home and hosted them impeccably. Some would become regular visitors and part of our lives. They would enrich our family and we would look forward to their return. Our children would benefit close up from their knowledge and wisdom and in many cases, saw a fantastically positive and private side of public figures. There was one particular Rabbi and historian who, like me, was an early-riser. We would sit on the patio, coffee in hand, as the sun rose, and so much would be illuminated. I also saw global icons contorted with stress and in rare moments of anxiety, lamenting that they were too old to be a failure – despite their perceived success. I was comforted by this, for indeed, we are all human. I was not the only one carrying a banner.

Some we would refuse to host again. I recall seeing one visitor leaving for the airport (when I thought that he was going the next day) and I confirmed he was indeed departing after staying the week. He was in fact difficult to host and didn't seem to appreciate much. He mentioned that I should please thank my wife for her hospitality. I replied, "she is home, you can thank her yourself if you want," and he answered that it was no problem; I could just thank her for him. He was, needless to say, never welcomed back and my children have been drilled on the importance of personal thank you's. Some visitors arrived with bag-loads of washing, assuming that as a South African home we would have more help than we know what do with, but we smiled and accepted their offerings.

We were close to our families. We lived in walking distance of our siblings, saw them weekly, and went on weekends away, cruises and multiple vacations together. We loved the time that we spent and buried the irritation that is part of being so enmeshed by focusing on the big picture.

My parents were the shepherds, keeping their flock together, defending their charges no matter whether the "threat" came from within or without. They placated and negotiated, worried and nurtured, and if need be, fought with the required aggression to ensure that the family remained whole. They valued family above all else and would pay any price to ensure that this bond remained unbroken, remained strong, at least on their watch.

In this environment I played the role that I was conditioned to play. I was strong, dependable, supportive and "real". I was not an easy personality, but I wore my success with charm and grace. As one friend would later remark – "every family should have at least one Howard."

The banner I held was impressive, but it was not sustainable.

Chapter Two

RAISING THE BANNER

COMMODITY TRADING IS all-consuming – it makes all else seem dull and commonplace. It is the trade-of-the-gods. Traders own the world. They become intimate with the major cities on our planet, know the hotels of choice, airline schedules, the latest trends and restaurants, clubs and cafés and fashion. There is an unspoken code of assessing one another. Watch, shoes and belts are the secret cues of communication and much is known about another even before shaking hands. It is a tight club, and the need to be part of it is primal.

Messages are sent and delivered on a continuous basis and you are graded accordingly. Conferences punctuate the year and although appear to be fun, are serious business. What happens on conference stays on conference – with alcohol abuse and debauchery having few limits.

This unrecorded "score chart" takes note of your every move. Did you travel by taxi or take the helicopter from the conference in Monte Carlo to the airport in Nice (even though the drive took the same amount of time); is your tie Hermès and your belt Ferragamo (until the Hermès belt with the H became the item of choice), is your suit Boss or Armani (little else would do unless it is custom made, but only in London and not by the tailors in Hong Kong, as everyone knows that they aren't up to par). Rolex is passé unless it is the Daytona. IWC is always acceptable, Hublot – too in your face, Cartier works and Panerai says "I have class, have money and I am aware of the latest trends". I had two. Sometimes a renegade would be wearing (and I mention this in a whisper) a Polo running watch. This "bourgeois badge" might unnerve everyone, but it bears an acceptable message: I might work hard but I am above the need to wear a fancy watch. Suits are slim-fit and preferably navy blue and shirts crisp white. Ties need to be skinny, unless you are not. Louis Vuitton luggage is "showy" unless plain black, although it is acceptable if you are Asian. Tumi roll-on, in black, with the briefcase that slides over the handle is a prerequisite. Check-in luggage is embarrassing and very uncool even though you have more weight allowance than God. It was Nokia then BlackBerry then iPhone and now it's Samsung. It was IBM and now it is MacBook Pro. It is the latest iPad. Pens are Montblanc although Lamy says you might know your stuff – and business card holders are to be used by the Chinese only. Your coat is Burberry. Your shoes Prada. But you feign indifference to it all. Caring too much is a fatal flaw. It is tantamount to sinking the black ball before any other. Everyone knows that.

What exists outside of this is too scary to contemplate. In order to remain on top of the game, one has to be hyper-vigilant, not miss a social cue or nuance. At a conference hotel you would need to party until 3 am and be at the gym at 6 am – even if this means sneaking off to your room for a quick nap in the afternoon – no one will know that you are not in a meeting. This pace is invigorating for those can keep up, but stressful beyond imagination for anyone not designed for the challenge. No matter the circumstances or how intimidating the crowd, your aim is to walk into a room full of strangers and walk out of a room full of friends. I loved it.

Whilst on family vacations at any given hotel, I would meet and befriend people from around the world. I spoke an international language and could communicate with anyone I chose. I was never tall or dark or handsome, but I attracted people on another basis that I have never fully understood. My family would marvel at how strangers would come and talk to me and how quickly I established common ground with unfamiliar people. I retained and added to a network that might never be linked to a field of business interest, but would use this network to connect others in the field, simply because I could. I have long examined my own motives and needs, and can find nothing sinister in what I did. Quite the contrary. It wrote me into their story and I thrived on that. Time and time zones demanded that I would let some of these relationships slide, but I knew that a phone call or an email would ignite them whenever required.

I recall sitting next to a stranger on a flight and knowing that he had a low sperm count before takeoff. This is naturally not a way to start a conversation with your neighbour seated in 1C, and I would not recommend one opens a discussion on this basis. As much as I enjoy getting to know people, I did become slightly unnerved at the ease in which that was disclosed to me, but was comforted by the thought that this had to be some kind of record. This normally takes me to at least Kenyan airspace to determine.

I "collected" people from around the world. I connected them to others in areas of common interest, and I enjoyed seeing what I had accomplished. I was not a financial snob and wasn't drawn to people simply by what they had amassed, but also by whom they were, their intellectual capability, notable achievements or potential. I made friends effortlessly as I was, and am, genuinely interested in people.

How close I allowed them to get to me was a different story and as I think back on this, I am really surprised that no one noticed. I allowed very few people in and saw vulnerability in myself, as weakness. The pattern was set for me and it was much easier to be the support rather than to be the one in need. I gave generously in all areas to my friends and didn't expect much back. When I did expect return support and it wasn't forthcoming to my standard, I became gravely disenchanted and disengaged, as I had done with my family. The truth is that I liked myself, but I wasn't always good for me.

Sleep was never easy for me, and so I dismissed it as having little value. I went to gym at 5 am every morning for years. Sleep was weakness. It was a mortal requirement and the further I could remove myself from that need, the more I could accomplish. I owned the early morning, which has always been my time of hope and possibility. It is the time where I can be true to myself and completely alone. But I always was able to work.

If I needed to go to the bathroom in the middle of the night, I would instinctively pick up my BlackBerry and read any emails that I had missed while sleeping. With China being six hours ahead and the US East Coast being six hours behind, with a workaholic partner and employees the same, there was never a time when there wasn't something to catch up on. To receive 400 emails a day was not abnormal. It became like a perpetual climbing treadmill where you needed to keep going in order not to fall back down. But you could never reach the top.

Through this, I retained real friendships and was the support that every friend and family member wanted and needed. I could sense vulnerability in a crowded room, and I was trustworthy and loyal. From early on I had developed a high EQ and was seldom wrong when it came to picking up on dynamics. People naturally confide in me and I would not betray their confidence. In many ways I liked what I had become.

I continued to read two or three books a week. Reading was my refuge, but I also liked what I could claim justifiably on my banner "Howard Feldman is in the global world of economic trade, and yet he finds the time to read". I became a one man bookclub with my novels circulating around the neighbourhood. On Shabbat, when I could not work, reading was something worthy to keep me occupied from 4 am when I woke up. Plus this was something that I could use to prove how "normal" I was. It was also what fed me and kept the small flame in my soul alive. I truly loved to read and was ruthless about what I consumed. I believed vehemently in Roland Barthes concept of the "Death of the Author", which meant that a text is a stand-alone work and holds no truth beyond what it presents to us. I read fiction, as it didn't present itself as anything but that. I loved the worlds created by words and got lost in the magical rhythms of prose. This meant for me that biographies were fiction along with almost anything else. In retrospect, it is interesting that I recoiled from the blatant banners that seem to saturate the many biographies and autobiographies I read. I had spent my life doing exactly the same.

One has to have some sense of self. I recognise that it is impossible for people not to hold up some kind of image. But I also believe that we don't need to present all (and sometimes not such attractive selves) to the world. I often tell my children that being in a bad mood just because you can be, is pollution. It sullies and destroys the atmosphere. It is unrealistic and unhealthy to have an insincere smile plastered permanently on your face, but we do have a social responsibility which includes not contaminating the environment. The balance between honesty and positivity is a delicate one and one where only we can know when we are presenting something that is ultimately going to hurt us.

Chapter Three

SCHOOL BAGS

I HOISTED MY banner early on in life. I grew up in a leafy suburb of Johannesburg. The third child of a well-respected Jewish family, I was pretty much left to my own devices. I was smart and horribly responsible. I realised from early on that I would need to make my own way. I knew I could not rely on the guidance of my parents, who although both born and bred South Africans, seemed to speak an entirely different language to me.

My father was a man I could not reach. We had no way of communicating – he being a rough-and-tumble sport guy, and me being more intellectual and emotionally intuitive. This fundamental difference meant that, try as we did, we could not find common ground. My almost obsessive interest in literature and the arts unnerved him and simply alienated us further. He did not (at that stage) value what I did and loved, and the message that I received over and over was that I had little value, at least to him.

My parents were the offspring of European refugees. Both were born in South Africa to lonely and displaced parents who were struggling to make sense of their new home. My father's parents came from Eastern Europe – my grandfather, moving to Pilgrim's Rest six years ahead of my grandmother as he didn't have the money for them both. Considering the state of their marriage as I remember it, I have often wondered if the poor old guy was simply enjoying the quiet life of a rural town before sending for his strong, dominant and dissatisfied wife!

Pilgrim's Rest was a village that sprung up after the discovery of what seemed to be a significant gold deposit in the late 1800s. It is situated in a magnificent but inaccessible North Eastern part of the country and was an active and busy hamlet until suddenly the gold ran out and it quite simply, died. It was perplexing how they landed up there, but at the time many Jews fleeing Europe would settle in destinations that would make very little sense to our generation. My grandfather was a man of deep religious knowledge and resource. He was a watchmaker and ran a small convenience store to eke out a living, but was also authorised to administer the kosher slaughter of chickens and was the cantor for his and other communities, especially on the High Holy Days.

Although he was committed to religious observance, as was common at the time, he was unsure as to how to pass this on to his two sons. His education back in Europe was religiously based as they were unable to go to regular schools but much of the instruction that he was given was harsh and unforgiving. It was a "fire and brimstone" approach to child rearing and I am certain that when he left this cold and harsh environment for the open and sunny skies of Africa, that along with the change of temperature came a change in attitude. He was not alone and many of his generation, confused by what was lifestyle and what was religious behaviour, failed to pass this on to their children. In my father's case, many traditions were upheld along with the flame of commitment until he would marry my mother and move back towards full observance.

My mother's parents came from Germany – both arriving as single, bereft people without any support. They had left their families in Germany and came to the only place that would provide them with an entry visa. They met and married, as it seemed the sensible thing to do. Their turbulent and passionate marriage lasted 60 years. When they died, they had built a legacy of three children, 15 grandchildren and more than 50 great-grandchildren.

It was not an easy marriage for my parents. The German sense of superiority and intellectualism did not mix well with the Eastern European superstitious way of life, and my parents got caught up in these East-West tensions. Understandably, both were damaged by their upbringing and brought enormous challenges into their marriage. It was never going to be a simple one and the constant conflict that typified their relationship was never easy for me to live with. I recall my mother turning to me one day and with reference to my father's Eastern European background, said, "It's really important that you marry someone from 'within'". To this

I responded, "But I thought dad was Jewish". So deep was this cultural divide.

Today there are many studies that examine the emotional impact on the offspring of survivors of the holocaust, but then no one understood this, or had the time and privilege to engage it. You simply survived it as best you could. As a result, I became hyper-vigilant, sensing the mood and atmosphere and monitoring every nuance. I assumed the role of my mother's protector – who although strong, was up against more than she could handle. I still remain perplexed by my childhood – it gave me the confidence and skills to conquer the world, and yet it was not secure and not what I would later want for my own children.

My grandparents were colourful characters. My German "Opa" and "Mommy Senta" were not the doting type. Although they tolerated us, and we would visit them every Saturday, they made no bones about the fact that we were not their favourite grandchildren.

Their approach to religious observance was one that I enjoyed. My grandmother was deeply religious and clearly turned to God for support when all else had failed her. She lost most of her family to the terrors of Europe as a young woman and took comfort in knowing that it was part of a greater albeit painful plan. She kept my grandfather, who was clearly somewhat of an eccentric, grounded and together they remained religiously observant and steadfast when it was not particularly popular to be so.

It would be my grandmother, who many years later, provided

the reality-check of real loss. On the night that we were emigrating and tears were flowing, she took me aside and told me that we all needed to pull ourselves together. She reminded me how she left Germany as a young woman of 19, knowing that she would never see her family again. She set sail, alone, to the tip of Africa where they spoke a language and embraced a culture that she would never fully understand.

They were also of the view that children should be seen (occasionally) and definitely not heard, and that most conversations were not for our tender ears. The command to "Go and look for the cats" meant my grandfather was going to tell a story that we were not to hear. Of course for us this meant that this was exactly the story we needed to find a way to have access to, as it probably would involve a description of their recent visit to a semi-naked beach in the South of France (along with a handheld first generation video for show and tell). Of course the lounge curtains that we peaked through would obscure much of the highly pixillated (and somewhat shaky) image on the screen, as the guy was no youngster and the stabiliser function had not been invented yet. But we got the picture.

It was from them that I learned the term "Blue Movies" and in fact it was with them that I would see the opening scenes of "1001 Erotic Nights". We were at Sun City and my sister and I wanted to see The Extravaganza. I was 14 and she was 18. When we went to book, my grandparents were in the front of the line and we asked them to buy tickets for us. They did so, and we sat with them in the theatre waiting for it to begin. I found it odd that there was a movie screen up but didn't take it too seriously until the lights went down, and the show began. It was then that I realised that they had taken us to see "a certain type of film". Needless to say we left hastily in shame and horror. No self-respecting teenager wants to sit next to his grandmother through entertainment like that – no matter how tempting! When I did comprehend what the show was, I turned to Mommy Senta, who was very obviously not surprised by the content, and said, in a high pitched querulous voice, "Is this not The Extravaganza?", to which she responded, with a slap on my leg, "Don't be silly, Hovard, it's a sexy movie!"

My father's parents came from Latvia. Well, in truth they were never quite certain as the borders were alleged to have changed many times during their lives. They were also not sure of their ages and declined to speak much of their past, but it was clear that it was no picnic. My grandfather was a gentle, kind man with a broad smile and endearing personality, my grandmother was an astute business woman, fiercely intelligent and the strength behind the marriage.

She considered me to be her favourite. So much so, that from a young age, she would lament how much she would like to be at my bar mitzvah, but unfortunately would be dead by then. She lived to 90, with a sharp and clear mind and all her faculties until the very end, but as a young child I was not to know that this was my first brush with advanced hypochondria. She did manage to pass away between my engagement and wedding, as though to prove her point, but I suspect that that was because she didn't like Heidi (following an incident with a bottle of L'Oréal hairspray, a teasing brush, an Eighties hairstyle and a severe asthma attack). She had a penchant for collapsing at the most inopportune moments and although we became accustomed to it, she continued to seek novel opportunities and venues.

When I was 15, for logistical reasons, I had to meet my parents in Cape Town where we were going on holiday. My parents asked if I would accompany my grandmother down to the coast, as it was difficult for her to travel alone. This was no problem for me as I was used to the role. We boarded the plane and all was well until my grandmother went to the toilet.

Shortly after that, I heard an announcement calling for a doctor on board. I tried to continue eating my tuna sandwich, but the empty seat next to me made me very uneasy. It was then that I leaned over and looked towards the back of the plane. There I saw two horribly familiar feet pointing upward. It needs to be mentioned that she also had a thing for having toes removed from time to time (something I have never been clear on) which made her feet unmistakable to any family member. I pushed my food aside and went to the back of the plane, convinced that it was not a serious situation, but also knowing that everyone would think it was. As I got closer I heard her familiar moaning "Oy, Oy, Oy" which only confirmed that she was not in peril. "Granny!" I said through clenched teeth, whilst nudging her shoe with mine (Ok, kicking her gently), "Get up! Just get up!" Needless to say the flight attendants, sweet young things, were mortified by my lack of sympathy and ushered me back to my seat so that they could take care of this grand old lady who had passed out in the galley.

When my parents watched the ambulance arrive at the planeside to assist with the disembarkation of an ill passenger, they had little doubt as to whom it was, and when they saw the look on my face as I walked towards them, it was confirmed.

With all this, my mother protected me like a warrior. As much as I looked after her, she did so with me, recognising that I was not the same as my siblings and that I had difficulties communicating with my father.

The primary school provided a school bus that was monitored by the Grade Six kids. One morning when I was in Grade Four, one of the monitors started hitting the younger kids with a stick. Even as a small child I had an inbred hatred of injustice and managed to take the stick away from the bully. But not before my name was written down.

It was also customary for the entire school to line up for announcements and uniform check before walking to class in single file. During the announcements the headmaster, a man I found to be unpredictable and unstable, called out my name for misbehaving on the bus. I was commanded to step forward and onto the stage.

It was clear that an example was to be made of me. Shaking with trepidation, I walked to the front of the hall and slowly climbed the steps to the stage. I walked towards him and felt the eyes of the whole school watching. He then asked me to turn to face the school. I registered fear on all their faces and I knew it was a reflection of my own anxiety.

Without a word he took the belt out of the trousers, made me bend over, and hit me as hard as he could manage. The first-graders were in the front row, and most had their hands over their mouths in horror. I was much older and needed to behave as such. I was eight years old after all. I didn't cry and somehow knew that I needed to retain as much dignity as I could manage until I got to my class, where I remember breaking down in the presence of my friends and classmates who were mortified by what had happened. I was infuriated by the terrible injustice of not being allowed to give my side of the story and, of course, by the humiliation.

I don't remember how I made it through the day, but when I got home that afternoon and told my mother, I did so with genuine anguish. I was traumatised.

She reacted immediately. "Get into the car!" she screamed at me and off we went to Yeoville to the apartment building where the headmaster and his family were known to live. She hadn't met him officially as he had recently come to South Africa from London, but this was not a time for formalities.

His wife answered the door and my mother calmly requested to see her husband. As politely as she could manage, the wife explained that he was lying down with a headache and couldn't be disturbed. There was no doubt that she had recognised the insane glint in my mother's eye and was intuitive enough to grasp that preventing this meeting might save lives.

At this point my mother could no longer contain her rage, pushed past her, stormed down the passage to where she assumed his bedroom was, flung open the door to find the man indeed lying in his bed. With that, she pulled the pillow from under his tender head and started beating him up in what must have been the most aggressive pillow fight of all time. She screamed all sorts of abuse at him, threatened his life if he ever laid a finger on me or anyone she knew or might get to know in the future, grabbed my hand as I cowered at the door and swept out of the apartment.

I have no idea whether my public flogging, or the vision of my mother beating up my principal, was more traumatic. Needless to say, he could not look me in the eye for the remainder of the year, after which I would leave that school, and my mother and his wife would go on to become best of friends. My mother had clearly done what his wife had wanted to do for years.

When my father came home that night and was told to discuss this with me, the conversation went roughly as follows, "Mom told me what happened to you at school today. I want you to forget about it. Ok?" And I agreed to. But I didn't.

To be fair, today my father is a very different person and our relationship a strong and connected one. He is uncomfortable by who he was and often speaks of my youth with real regret. We are open and honest, recognise our differences and enjoy a real connection. But this would take many years and considerable work. Recently he told me that at 78 he has made a decision to focus on the present, enjoy each moment while he is healthy, do as much good as he can do for those around him, not look back as it is often painful, not look forward as we have no idea what the future holds, but be present, appreciative and conscious.

Almost as a defense mechanism, and in order to cope with my

perceived rejection of my father, I decided that I simply didn't belong in the family, that I was different to the rest and that if I was to make my way in the world I would have to be independent. It was a childish way to avoid the terrible pain of that ultimate rejection, but I knew that I had only myself to rely on and would prove that I didn't need them. But parents count, whether we like it or not, and so I would spend the next 40 years trying to make them notice. These notions were obviously not conscious ones and it was only when I stopped trying to prove that I had intrinsic value that I could think about why I would do so. In my mind, I might have been born a disappointment, but I would not live as one.

But the flip side of this independence was recognition that I was different to the rest of my family. Although today the family gene is unmistakable, as a child I didn't look the same as my siblings and this exacerbated the feeling of isolation. I found comfort in books and plays on the radio (we didn't get TV in South Africa until 1976). My mental strength developed and I developed cognitive skills that they are teaching today in CBT. I recall so clearly as a schoolboy lying in bed dreading the day ahead. Within minutes I would find something to look forward to, move on from there to ways in which I was going to change the world and I would rise with purpose and energy to face the day.

Anyone who has experienced a Johannesburg winter knows that it is deceiving. The sun shines for 5 months and there is rarely rain. But it is cold, very cold; especially in the early mornings when the icy Highveld wind can drop the 0°C early morning start down to -4° or -5°C. Our school uniform for the winter consisted of a white shirt and school tie, grey school jersey and dark grey blazer. This was to be matched with either long or short grey trousers. If you wore short pants, you needed to wear the designated grey and red school socks. We wore short pants, because as my father so eloquently put it, "Only the sissy-boys wore longs." I can still picture the goose bumps on my legs as we sat waiting outside for the school bus. I recall pulling my socks up as high as I was able to protect myself from the chill, until I could see the bus in the distance and would hastily pull them into their rightful position before the bus arrived. I would then board, glancing enviously at the "sissies" who were allowed to wear long pants in winter.

I also found that the only way to cope in my environment was to be punctual and orderly. This was not simple given the friendly chaos in which we lived. We were never the neat lunchbox types at school and our sandwiches, left over chicken with a soup ladle of gravy hastily wrapped in a Checkers packet would stain and pollute everything in my bag. My shame and revulsion at unpacking these lunches would stay with me forever and I would stare enviously at the neat sliced carrots that fitted snugly in my friends' lunchboxes, alongside a juice bottle that I never owned. It needs to be said that my friends soon caught on to this and offered to buy my sandwiches, clearly made with love and abundance. This was most likely my first commodity of trade!

It is no wonder that the moving house experience at age 13 is a memory that stays with me.

To put it in perspective, we moved from number 172 to 187 Frances Street, a big move for people who were afraid of change (little wonder I spent so much of my adult life moving continents). This was not easy for my parents who found it difficult to agree on much, but they finally undertook this massive move.

Rather than engaging movers (my father found them a miserable waste of money), he sent a few Bedford trucks from his factory to assist in the honour. My mother, not the most organised person, spent the last few hours throwing anything and everything into bags and boxes (collected from various outlets). It was like the exodus out of Egypt without the miracles to bring it all together.

To add to this, my father had recently snapped his Achilles tendon and was more difficult than normal as he hobbled about on crutches in pain and in temper. My siblings, more skilled at the art of doing nothing and keeping out of harms way, did exactly that, whilst I went to my room in the new house, unpacked all my boxes, made my bed and started to put up my paintings and posters. My room was a bastion of serenity in a sea of chaos and I was particularly proud of my achievement that day. The view over the Observatory golf course was pleasing and I knew I could make this a haven.

My father did not see it the same way. When he walked into my room the look that he gave me was like he had caught me doing drugs, having used the new curtains as a tourniquet. He lost it, screaming something about the rest of the family not having beds while I was putting the finishing touches on my decor. To this day, I feel misunderstood. I wonder why he could not see that the only way that I could make sense of my life was to take charge of it.

Our house was a busy one, and although I didn't rate many of my parents' friends (so many of them seem to bask in army stories), I learned social skills that would be useful and vital for a lifetime. My parents were people who would welcome anyone in need and assist however they could and although their brand of marriage and housekeeping and child rearing was not to be mine, I have to acknowledge that the essence of kindness, justice, loyalty and love that I gleaned, would add to who I became.

And so I asked for nothing. I did my schoolwork, excelled in many areas, was very social, won numerous awards in public speaking and drama and managed to be chosen Head Boy. And because I managed without need, it was determined that I was to be "trouble-free motoring" as was the byline of an advert at the time. I lived that role with conviction. I became the turn-to guy, Mr Dependable, the award-winner. My success finally meant recognition. I held up the banner in order to be noticed. And it worked.

The pattern was established. Off to university to study a Bachelor of Arts with Law and English Literature as majors, then on to my LLB where I was elected as a member of the Law Student Council (in fact the first non-racial LSC of Wits University) and finally Editor of the Law Review.

And so, my banner was raised.

Chapter Four

HOLDING THE BANNER WHEN THE SOUTH EASTER BLOWS

HEIDI AND I met in Muizenberg outside Cape Town. She was 16 and had just returned from a three-week sleep-away day camp. I was 19, had just completed my first year at university and was on holiday with my family.

My parents had very specific routines in terms of vacations and each year we would spend 4 weeks in the area. Many people have wonderful memories of Muizenberg with its olde-world hotels, broad promenade, warm waters and Archie-comic social scene. It apparently peaked in the 1950s and 1960s and had become a little anachronistic over the last five decades. It was very popular amongst the Jewish community, and even had been dubbed "Jewsenburg" – for obvious reasons.

Imagine the scandal when one of the kosher hotels, The Sharon, relinquished its roots and heritage and changed its name to become, rather brazenly I think, The Shrimpton (a shrimp being a notoriously un-kosher delicacy). It was all we spoke about for at least three Friday night dinners, but never in front of my grandmother who was aging and who stayed there every year. To her it was and always would be The Sharon. She was of the opinion that the food had actually improved over the years. But let's not go there.

It was also a place where a home-proud mom could show off her family, her home making skills and discuss the bright future of her three-year-old, the future doctor, as he played in the safe warm waters. Moms battled other moms for domination, all with broad smiles and lilting voices, whilst their husbands glistened and baked their rounded and satisfied bellies, smeared in tanning oil (with protection factor two). They were blissfully ignorant of what was really going on around them as they fried and roasted their European pale skin (and prepared for melanomas some years later). Food underscored any conversation, and if the beach was the battleground, food was the weaponry of this cold war – perhaps even more vicious and deadly than that raging between the USA and the Soviet Union at the time.

Admittedly, no one would be born with three arms, as in the case of threatening nuclear fallout, but three chins became all too common. Many generations following would battle the effects of obesity, high cholesterol, diabetes, metabolic syndrome and plain ugliness.

This was a time before sushi went viral and "carbs" were demonised. So eating everything was an option, with chicken being the ammunition of choice. I have no doubt that considering the volume of roast chickens consumed on its shores, archeologists in a few hundred years, on discovering the disproportionate number of drumstick chicken bones, will be wondering if it was perhaps a poultry breeding area. The abundance of food sadly had a real and significant effect on how the general populace looked in their swimming gear and this trend continued over the years. It is small wonder that the younger set "upped" and went to "the other side" of the mountain where the more trendy and in-vogue Clifton and Camps Bay beaches were situated.

Over the years, Muizenberg has decayed, with fewer and fewer people choosing it for their annual holiday. Even the weather seems to have deteriorated – the wind, cold and angry, seems to blow through the summer months too. A good day now lasts a few hours and is defined by the opportunity to sit on the beach "behind the huts" which act as a windbreaker. If you do want to drive through from the "other side" it is advised not to stop for petrol – those extra ten minutes could mean the difference between managing to get onto the beach, or not.

But those that still do go, love it and defend it and do not accept any criticism of it. It is a banner that they struggle to hold when the South Easter blows, but with almost religious fervour, defend it they do. I recall the look of horror one day when we did drive through from "the other side" and I casually mentioned that I should have packed a toothbrush to assist extracting the sand from my teeth. The response was not cordial, but then I couldn't really hear it clearly as I had so much sand in my ears.

But Muizenberg remains of significance for many who met first girlfriends, boyfriends, spouses, and cemented friendships on its beach. Heidi and I could add our meeting to the lists of those who had met in the place where the wind would blow and blow, and although we ceased vacationing there many years ago, we are grateful for this little town on the Indian Ocean.

It was an arranged marriage of sorts, although neither of us would know that, and our mothers' claiming ownership of this would continue to annoy Heidi for the 23 years we have been married. Both my mother and Heidi's mother share German roots. Their parents were friends and even might have been family back in Europe and although they had drifted, were still very much part of each other's lives. In fact, our grandfathers clearly didn't see eye to eye and were openly hostile to each other, which meant there might even have been more history than we would ever know. But our mothers were used to getting what they wanted and without saying so, it was clear that they both liked the idea of this union. And so they went to work. Their plan was simple – create opportunity for interaction as frequently as possible and we would have no option but to fall hopelessly in love.

Holidays were only a couple of weeks long, and so they had a short time to make this happen. We met at the quintessential South African social gathering – a braai (barbeque). What I best remember from that evening is trying to get out of the wind, debating how to keep the steaks from flying off the grill and also sensing that I had met someone who had the potential to alter the course of my life. Heidi was shy and strong and had dignity, strength, refinement and wisdom at 16. We were drawn to one another then, and we have never looked back.

After that, the mothers fabricated a range of domestic crises or opportunities for us to cross paths. My mother ran out of potatoes and I had to go and borrow some. Then borrowed potatoes had to be returned, and I was asked to do so. And then the family came for dinner and then we kept bumping into them wherever we went. It was the strangest thing. Almost like it was meant to be. And in fact it was. As these two matriarchs had decided it, so it would be.

The relationship was a natural and easy one. Both our first loves, we were undamaged and unburdened by past hurts. We went out for three years and got engaged very young, to the shock and horror of many around us, and got married 8 months later. At our wedding I sang the song "Almaz" as it speaks of the "love that innocence brings". And indeed for us, it did.

Luckily for me, this proved to be the best decision of my life and after 23 years and 5 children, I can say with real contentment that I did that for me and for us, and for no one else.

There was little chance of achieving any success if Heidi wasn't at my side. Her support, strength, love and devotion, along with her uncomplicated belief in God, has been the constant in my life. She believes that whatever we experience we do for a reason and it is up to us how to deal with it, make the best of it and introspect. She is convinced that we are in this world for a purpose and if we don't harness and achieve it, it is a wasted opportunity. Although I am a maverick and a bit of a loner, she has managed to balance this all allowing me to explore and dream and take risks and journey in search of my Ithaca, knowing that I have had a solid base and a rock to which I can always swim back.

Still, back then, this was an excellent addition to the banner. I had met a highly acceptable girl from a highly acceptable family and we fell in love and got married and everyone approved. I had value, as I continued to prove that I could be the prodigal son.

Chapter Five

IN SEARCH OF AN ASTOUNDING CAREER

DURING MY TIME at law school, I became fascinated by mining law which was undergoing an evolution along with many other South African laws. I was privileged to be at Wits University, and at law school, at the birth of our democracy, when we became the "rainbow nation" and anything was possible. None of the leaders had had the time to disappoint us as they would do later, and our unwritten Constitution was a blank canvas on which anything could be painted. It was also an uncertain time, for no one knew what indeed the future would hold and how middle-class white males would fare in such a place. But those were not our worries – they were the worries of the older, fearful and skeptical generation who had been schooled in the notion of the "Swartgevaar" (the Black danger).

In fact, my parents were desperately worried that I was going to become a "liberal" at Wits, which could mean all sorts of very scary things for them. In truth, it was a dangerous time with State of Emergency in place and the riot police a constant feature of university life. We very often stood at the top of the buildings watching them chase and bludgeon students as they ran screaming, or sat in the library and listened to the stampede as it passed us by. No one knew who was part of the secret police and parents worried anxiously that their children were getting caught up in a world that would lead to detention-without-trial, or worse. It was all very well to know that apartheid had to end, but many didn't want their children involved.

But we were young, had our future ahead of us and believed in the inherent good of our fellow South Africans. Of course we had also been through a schooling process that demanded we learn the "Advantages of Separate Development", but it was made clear that we learn those concepts simply in order to cover the syllabus, and that no self-respecting Jewish person could really endorse this concept. Who could not recall with horror the oversized police vans driving through our white neighbourhood checking "passes" of any black person they encountered? Who could forget the fear as those who didn't have a "pass" would run, often chased, hiding in any place our area would allow – often in our own home with the assistance of my parents? For who could condone such a ubiquitous and inhumane law? But with the change, came unnerving and nagging doubts. What if they were right? So we were one step more evolved than our parents and our future held promise.

It was also a time of upheaval, as many childhood friends contemplated and ultimately left the country for a more certain future. My group in particular, went to Melbourne, Australia, where they seem to have led acceptable and stable lives. Their heart rates remain constant at 75 beats per minute and they continue to insist that they made the right choice. Perhaps they did, but my hope is that in their private moments they, too, are able to put down the banner and wonder, with honesty, if it was worth it.

My father-in-law ran a mining company. I was a lawyer, and I had studied mining law, so it followed that I would join the company. During my time there, I became increasingly close to him and learned a tremendous amount about the industry. The value in working for a small privately-owned mining company is that you get to learn all aspects of the business.

From malfunctioning winches, to "dirty mining", yields and recoveries, to processing plants, labour issues, logistics, shipping, documents, quality control and, of course, sales. One needs to understand it all. Later on, when Metalmin was born, this would become invaluable – I would know and understand not only if we were being ripped off, but understand the challenges that the producers face.

Most miners (except maybe not at the bottom of the commodity cycle when cash dominates everything) prefer to sell to someone who understands the products and the challenges of production. When expectations are real, there are fewer comebacks and a lot less aggravation. It therefore became critical to understand the chemistry of these products and I would later surprise our young guys by looking at a Certificate of Analyses and pointing out a mistake, as there was no way, for example, that the SiO2 could be the result being reflected if the Cr2O3 was reflecting the same. It would also tell me which reef was being mined and if the product could indeed come from the area that they purported it did. More so than in most businesses, in the physical trade sector, knowledge is king and not having it is very, very expensive.

One of the more tedious tasks was managing the Mining Licenses, Environmental Impact Study and working with the Department of Mineral and Energy Affairs. As South Africa struggled to find its path in a post-apartheid world, the balance between maximisation of its valuable resources, encouraging the miners and investors and addressing some issues created by the past legacy, this department in particular, has found it difficult to find its feet, and indeed to achieve a balance. Important, yet ultimately futile debates raged of legislated beneficiation, where mines would be precluded from exporting ore. Mines were in fact forced, either by a punitive tax or quota system, to beneficiate it into a more refined product (when there would not be enough power to do so in any event), an aged and confused railway system. There was a need to have First World Environmental policies, but without the infrastructure to support it, corruption, cronyism, lack of training would all frustrate and exasperate even the most optimistic investors. Add to this a 26 per cent BEE ownership component and no one knows quite what they are doing.

What fascinated me most, were the markets and the international trade aspect of the business. So when I was approached and offered a position at Glencore, with my father-in-law's blessing, I seized the opportunity. Of course it was not as simple as that, and my interviews took place in Johannesburg and Zug, where I was sent from person to person, doing their best to unnerve me to see how I would cope under pressure. After meeting the various traders, I would then still have to meet with the Head of Alloys and then the Head of Coal.

This was extremely difficult for me, but I must have done acceptably as I was offered the position the following day. In standard Glencore style, I was given 24 hours to accept the offer. The plan was for me to be trained in Johannesburg and then move to Zug where I would work for the head of the Nickel department.

Shortly after I joined though, the Nickel Head left the company and I was at a loose end. I was placed on the FerroAlloys desk and learned to trade these products. The trade aspect came naturally to me, as did the concept that this business was all about relationships. I genuinely like and enjoy people, so this felt less like work and more like fun. I was not the guy to take clients to clubs (and nor would I ever be), but connected on a real level. However, the Glencore environment was not for me. It was a place where your body and soul were owned by the company and although you were rewarded accordingly, it was a pact I was unable to make. And whereas I might have done exactly that later on, Faustus was still clear in my mind and I couldn't bring myself to "sign in blood".

Mobile phones had not yet come to South Africa. I recall with amazement how the young trainees would stay late at the office, often with nothing to do, perhaps reading magazines, waiting for a call from Zug. If it was Ivon Glazenberg (then Head of Coal) or Roy Issakow (then Head of Alloys) and you got to answer the call, then you had hit the jackpot. These were the guys that would be responsible for making that critical decision to move you to Switzerland or elsewhere, as the case may be.

When the decision was made, the trader would have to pack up and go in an instant – you would be required to get to the location of choice as quickly as possible. This was naturally more complicated for those with families. Wives might have to give up jobs and children needed to be taken care of. On many occasions a family might be told that they were being moved, would sell their houses and consolidate their lifestyle, only to be told that they were not going anywhere. This was normally a sign to start looking elsewhere for employment.

Telex was the mode of communication and each department's trade would be printed in a different colour. These would be distributed to everyone and it was not unusual for the entire office to read of someone's humiliation in a telex.

There was nothing gentle or New Age about this environment and you were either tough enough to deal with it, or you were not. It was a boys' high school – cliques were formed, the strongest led and the weak were ridiculed. It was an environment of bullies. It was not uncommon for the young traders to listen in horror as their seniors would be sworn at and abused from afar.

I recall from that period one such incident with a fellow trainee, who had joined at the same time as I had. He had held a fairly senior position at a well-recognised bank, but had always wanted to be a trader. He had applied and managed to secure the position, and was being trained in what was called "Traffic". He was not a strong personality, and this was recognised very early on. He was also married and it was clear from conversations that his wife was close to her father, his father-in-law. I remember with such clarity the head of Alloys in Johannesburg publicly presenting him with the following hypothetical situation. "A boat is sinking, with you, your wife and her father on board. There is only space for her and one more person in the lifeboat. Tell me, who do you think she would choose to be saved – you or her father?" The trader sadly knew the answer all too well, but his mistake was to show that it hurt him. It was vulnerability and it was weakness, and allowing anyone to see it was simply stupid. It could then be exploited, and indeed it was. He was asked this question, amongst others with the same theme, every few days, until he finally gave it all up and went back to the bank.

Luckily, I managed to go through school as neither a bully nor a victim, and I like to think that I continued to manage in the same way in this environment. It was the time of sanction-busting and a name change at Glencore. Past misdeeds were spoken about in whispers, but also in awe. Marc Rich had started all this and we all wanted to be him.

Young South African men made good traders. It was an attractive field as it presented a way out of the country, it was sexy and it gave young men a lifestyle which they could only dream of. But you needed to know what you were signing up for. In an article on the Glencore/Xstrata merger, Glazenberg stated very clearly "We don't do work-life balance". It is that simple. You either sign up for it, or you don't.

One Sunday afternoon, when attending my young nephew's birthday party, I received a phone call to say that I had to be in Walvis Bay urgently to view a Manganese Ore stockpile. There was no time to waste, so I hastily said goodbye to Heidi and our young son, Zac, went home to get my things and dashed to the airport, just making the last flight out to Namibia.

A few hours later along with another young colleague, we arrived at our destination. There was no one to show us to the mine, which in fact was not operational, and there was no one to point us in the direction of the stockpile. It was an exercise in futility and there was certainly no urgency associated with this trip.

With a sinking realisation that this was a ploy to claim ownership of us and our time, it just didn't feel right for me. The entire trip turned out to be a waste of time. In order to keep busy, we took a drive to Swakopmund, an old German town in the area, and sat at the docks watching the dolphins in the bay – it was really beautiful and peaceful and it gave both of us time to contemplate. It was dark when we drove along the desert road back to Walvis Bay and I had never seen an evening quite as spectacular. We pulled over to the side of the road, switched off the headlights and looked up to the heavens. The night sky was the most magnificent view I had ever seen. I was filled by a sense of what lay ahead, and I knew then that the road I was on was not the one I wanted to travel. My colleague resigned the day we returned, I did so a week later.

And so the idea of starting a commodity company was born. I could trade. My father-in-law's company had product, we employed a trader we knew and respected, and we called the company Metalmin. Initially the products that we traded were those supplied by the family mines. The tonnages were low and the conflict between the mine and trading company was clearly going to be an issue. The focus was Chrome foundry sand and some other low volume products, as China was not awake yet and the demand for South African metallurgical chrome outside of the country hardly existed. A new chapter had begun.

And then, not for the first time, it would all change.

Chapter Six

TAMPERED LUGGAGE

OUR APARTMENT IN Killarney was beautiful – large and airy with pale pink shades and beautifully decorated. The views over the North of Johannesburg were spectacular. The urban forest in all its magnificence stretched before us. When the summer arrived, the world turned purple and the jacaranda trees bloomed, it seemed, for our viewing pleasure. I was completing my LLB, whilst we were supported by our families and we were truly blessed. Friends would often use our home as a base for learning, which made one particular night in October uneventful. I do recall that a group of LLB friends were trying to make sense of Accounts 101, something that does not come naturally to most law students, and we worked through this unfathomable subject until late that night.

Little did we know that while we were trying to understand

the basics of debits and credits, a few blocks away, Heidi's grandmother was being tortured and murdered.

Heidi's grandparents lived in a breathtaking home that has become an icon in the Johannesburg suburb of Houghton. It was designed and built in the late 1950s with many of the materials being imported from Europe. It was underlaid with copper pipes that pumped hot water and warmed the house in winter, and the magnificent high ceiling would keep it cool in the summer. Its majestic white columns and circular driveway was testimony to the material success of its inhabitants – the imported Cadillacs that would often be poised outside the front door, the finishing touch. The interior, as well as the exterior was absolutely breathtaking and I will never forget my first visit to the house. The art, the marble, the antique furniture were magnificent beyond anything that I had seen.

There was no security wall around the property, despite my in-laws futile insistence that they build one and the magnificent sash windows were unhindered by bars. Access was not difficult and break-ins became more frequent.

The belief is that the perpetrators were in the house many hours before the elderly couple were confronted, and sat patiently in the study waiting for the right moment. The next few hours can only be imagined with horror.

I remember so vividly answering the phone at 6:15 am and trying to process the news. I gently woke Heidi and told her what I knew and that we needed to get dressed and go to the scene of the murder. I recall her standing at the mirror debating which earrings matched with what she was wearing. It perplexed me, but when your world is falling apart, sometimes the image that we present and the rituals we perform become more important to keep it all together. Looking back I now understand that it is hard to lower a banner, even under extreme circumstances.

The scene was brutal. The stench of blood, the splattered walls from her slashed carotid artery, disturbed us more than can ever be imagined. No one seemed too worried about contaminating the scene and I recall gingerly stepping between the massive pools of blood that seemed to be everywhere.

The house had been ransacked and the content of drawers and cupboards were scattered throughout. The scene was one of devastation. I remember thinking that if this scene was in a movie, I would dismiss it as being non-authentic, so extreme was the chaos. The Daimler was missing from the garage, and would later be found scrubbed clean of all evidence in Hillbrow, a rundown urban suburb of Johannesburg.

Heidi's grandmother still lay in the house. During the attack, her grandfather had been beaten and handcuffed to the balustrades at the bottom of the stairs. In a bizarre act of "mercy" the perpetrators had brought a chair for him to sit on. How could anyone be so brutal, and to old people, and yet perform what can only be an act of "kindness"? When we got to the house he had not yet been taken to hospital. He sat where he had been placed the night before, now covered with a sheet that someone had thrown over him. He was dazed and bewildered, as indeed we all were. "I have been calling her," he kept repeating, as though it was a mantra, "but she doesn't answer." He knew then that she was dead.

It was as slow as it was surreal, and no one seemed to know how to act under the circumstances. In search of something useful to do, we accompanied him when he went to the hospital. He was lucid and conscious and we spoke vaguely about the incident. He then went silent and never spoke of it, or anything else again. A year later, he died. It happened to be that I was the one called to be with him when he passed on, held his hand and said the Prayer for the Dying as he slipped away, lay him on the floor as is customary, lit a candle and waited for the Jewish Burial Society to arrive, not leaving him alone. My second son, Benjamin bears his name.

My father-in-law (it was his mother), was on a flight back from Europe and hadn't heard the news, and my mother-in-law and Heidi's uncle and aunt (who lived next door) were left to deal with it all. In desperation she called my parents and they arrived to assist. In a crisis they are always there and their presence is a comfort to those in need. They were there then, and they were indeed a comfort to her.

The situation was unreal. This was a grandmother, the person whose shoes my Heidi would play with as a little girl, whose jewellery she would try on, who she would go shopping with. It is her food that she dreams of and its her recipes she wants. And now she had been murdered and no one understood why.

The theories came thick and fast, each more wild and ludicrous than the next. We would never find out the truth, and in all honesty I can't see what difference it makes. I don't believe that the family would have achieved closure from this, as they would have a horrible and painful journey to go through, no matter what. I know this is an unpopular theory, but when I would later experience my own assaults, I remained true to this and would have no desire or need for the perpetrators to be apprehended. It might have been that I viewed most of the people in my world as criminal – unhealthy I know – but for me it made, and continues to make no difference whether they are punished or not.

As a security precaution we were required to move out of our apartment until motives were established and the police could be sure that the rest of the family was not at risk. We had no time to go back during the day, so returned that night. It so happened that during that October, the many flats in the building were being renovated and there were very few residents present. The building felt empty and dangerous and every step seemed to echo off the walls of the lobby, which was covered in scaffolding and repair materials. I entered the apartment accompanied by security, to collect essentials for us. Our pink apartment was now dark and I was instructed not to turn on any lights and to move as quickly as possible, take what we needed and leave. We were allowed back home a few days later when it was clear that no progress was going to be made and that no one else was at risk.

The cocoon that we had created as a newly-wed couple didn't feel that safe any more and the light in which we basked, dimmed. My wife's family emigrated and we remained.

Chapter Seven

PACKING AND UNPACKING

METALMIN CONTINUED TO plod on. With the focus of the family shifting abroad, selling assets and disinvesting, the drive to create a successful business had dissipated. I was a 20 per cent shareholder and back to being more active in the mining company. Therefore I had little say as to the direction of the trading company. Our head trader was solid, but would always remain a one-man show – he would never be able to build a team and work with others. His style was old-school – spending most of his energy hiding the identity of his suppliers and customers. This was the accepted modus operandi of many traders at the time, in a world before the Internet and before real-time information. It meant that, as a good trader, if you were prepared to go to any developing region – Africa, Russia, South America and spend the time, develop the trust and the relationships, you would be able to control that product and sell it to Europe and the US at a magnificent return. Nothing would be as lucrative as this trade, and so it just didn't seem worthwhile for anyone to expand offerings or deepen range. When Russia opened up the goose would die and they would close their business. In some ways we would make the same mistake years later.

The success of this model relied on the separation of supplier and consumer, and if this was not possible, then at the very least, control over the supply chain. The model was only sustainable in a pre-Internet world as access to information in rural areas was limited. Control of this information was paramount. But as the world began to change, even the most rural supplier would have access to global pricing, could do the math and work out the cost of logistics and delivery. It was no longer sustainable. More so for the New York commodity traders, who were geographically disadvantaged. Many would continue to function on this basis and slowly they would disappear one by one. Buying product from Africa to sell to Europe no longer made sense and there was room for another South African trading company, based where most of the suppliers were. But it would take another few years and I still had an interesting detour to take.

After two years of marriage, our first son Zac was born. He was a bright, well-behaved, responsive child and was conditioned very early on to conform to our requirements. He was a sponge and soaked up everything that we doused him with. We made parenthood seem easy and I remember that at a mere six days old, we took him with us to meet friends for coffee on a Sunday morning as we always did. We didn't need a nurse, had very little help and held that banner with pride. Maybe we would tweak a few things when we had our next child, but we pretty much had it down pat. That is if you ignore the fact that he stuttered at two years, primarily as a result of the pressure we placed on him and the expectations we had for him to perform.

And then, nine months after the passing of Heidi's grandfather, Ben was born. He was hard to love. He undermined our confidence, pushed us to the edge and beyond, and was unrelenting in his misery. We could not comfort him.

We had recently bought and moved into a house in Glenhazel, a suburb of Johannesburg. Although the stand was large, the house was not. It consisted of 3 bedrooms, a living room, dining room and large playroom. What sold us on the house was the quaint "cottage feel" as well as the garden with its majestic trees, lush lawns and tranquillity. The bird life was spectacular and the colours of the garden were gorgeous.

That is until we decided to buy a golden retriever puppy. Simba went to work very quickly securing his position on the inside of the house by eating the washing machine (well, parts of it) and then setting his eye on the fridge. He swiftly took ownership of the outside and in no time we were prisoners indoors. He meant well, I think, but definitely was suffering from severe ADHD, something that we would learn a lot about later.

If by chance we would venture into the garden, Simba would stalk stealthily and then pounce with a roar that befitted his name, preferably on a child who would scream while being pinned to the ground and being buried in the dirt. He made our lives a living hell and I knew he needed to go. But Heidi hates failure and didn't give up so easily. So, when I was at work and distracted, in the midst of a Union negotiation and Heidi called to say we had an appointment for the dog and that I needed to be home by 5 pm, I readily agreed. My assumption was that it was with someone who had space in his oversized vehicle and would be taking him to the farm I had dreamed of. I was incorrect.

Instead what confronted me was a rather basset-looking woman, most definitely in need of a Friday at the parlour, who looked at me disdainfully, as bassets can. She was apparently a "dog psychologist". She didn't break eye contact with me and whispered, "Don't look at him, he knows we are talking about him". She was, of course referring to Simba, who by this stage was dismantling, bite by bloody bite, the metal security doors in order to make contact with the mongrels who had been brought along to "socialise" him. (Apparently we had failed to do this.) The look I gave Heidi was not one of love and respect, and we both knew that we would deal with this later (but not in front of Simba of course).

Not willing to waste the R500 that Heidi had already spent on this charlatan, we sat on the couch and spoke about Simba's childhood. I kid you not – you can't make this stuff up. I wondered, not for the first time if perhaps a little adversity might put a stop to all the drivel. I pictured my grandparents, who had fought to make ends meet, to keep their family together and who mourned a loss they would never come to terms with, and I realised that perspective is fleeting and visible when real priorities are under threat. We all know that attending a tragic funeral, loss of a child or a young parent, makes us appreciate our own, but that feeling is brief. I often wonder why so many people are drawn into other people's misery and need to be part of an event that is not theirs, and I wonder if it isn't because it allows us for a time, to have real perspective and real clarity. And in the interim, we empathised with Simba and spent a moment identifying with the separation anxiety that he must be feeling.

It was during the siege of Simba that one of Heidi's sisters came to visit us in Johannesburg, met her future husband the day before Ben's scheduled birth and never left. She lived with us for a few months and tolerated his screaming as she slept on a mattress on the floor next to his cot. She lived through the only "Ferberisation" we would attempt with any of our children and I am pretty sure she would never do the same with hers. It needs to be said, that so difficult was this child, that we would either sleep train him or beat him, so incessant was his screaming. In fact, I remember going on holiday and not getting into bed once that night as I sat in the lobby of the hotel and allowed Heidi and Zac to get some rest. Today he is a remarkably evolved and compassionate person and continues to challenge us and everything around him, in an intelligent and intuitive manner, but back then … well I can't say that I liked him very much.

After much contemplation we made the decision to follow the family to Israel and we lived there for three years. My wife had lost five sisters (one had returned) and her parents to emigration (she is the oldest of six girls), and the pull to be with family was strong. We had two young sons at the time and we felt that it was an opportune time to join them. I would continue to work in the mining business and would manage and travel as and when needed.

We had managed a few reconnaissance trips and found a lovely home in the area we were looking for. We prepared, packed and set off on an adventure that would cover a few continents and take five years to return us to a house two doors away from the one we had left. In fact, when we did come back and were unpacking, one of the movers commented that he remembered packing us up some years before. To this, my sister, who had come to assist quipped, "Yes, this couch is better travelled than most people I know."

Chapter Eight

PITCHING A BANNER IN HEBREW

WE LIVED IN Ra'anana, outside Tel Aviv – a village, but an international melting pot. Many people who live there are highly educated, travel extensively and have given up enormous opportunity in their native lands in order to fulfill their dream of living in Israel. Many do live with one eye on their place of birth, noting the financial success of their contemporaries.

I found the international feel to be refreshing and interesting and very much a fresh contrast to the parochial world that I had left. I remember sitting around a lunch table at some friends, remarking at the diversity of the crowd, hailing from Israel, Sweden, Canada, the UK, South Africa and then a "country" I had never heard of – Woodmere. It turned out to be a suburb of New York that doesn't only consider itself to be an independent state, but in fact the entire world. We would later live there for a year and it's a pity that the comment hadn't set off alarm bells and made us reconsider our decision.

Israel is a harsh environment. Just as South Africans cannot forget that they live at the tip of Africa, so one cannot ignore that Israel is in the Middle East. I worked internationally, spoke English all day and was protected from many of the local challenges, but Heidi was not. She needed to confront the teacher, the banktellers, and the drivers.

The indiscernible education system did leave us a bit battered. When Zac came home from kindergarten one day and asked if he could take an atlas to school to prove to his teacher that Egypt was in Africa and not in Asia as she had explained, we did have concerns. When they told us he was dyslexic in First Grade (but had completed Harry Potter in the original) we were even more so. But I was comforted by the fact, and I repeated this to Heidi, that every Israeli that we had ever met (and granted we didn't meet a lot in Ra'anana), clearly knew everything. That being the case, how bad could the education system be?

We, on the other hand, were slow learners. I recall one evening after we had been there for about three months saying how strange it was that we had not seen an account or bill. We double-checked some of the information that we had given to relevant accounts people and it was indeed correct. And then a thought hit me. Without saying a word, I walked out of the front door and down the driveway to our post box, which by this stage was crammed to capacity with mail. It had never occurred to us that we would have to clear the postbox ourselves, and that there wasn't a person to make it magically appear on the hall table. We clearly had a lot to learn.

And we did. What we did not become was ex-South Africans. Why is it that South Africans are the only people in the world who refer to themselves as "Ex"? If you ask an American who has lived abroad for 20 years outside of the USA, he will say he is an American. A Brit is a Brit, but a South African is an Ex-South African. It's almost a divorce or emotional break up that is painful. What follows is an animosity towards the country of birth. They relish and disseminate the negative stories of the country as if to prove to themselves and others why their move was justified and correct. It's a little sad really.

It is not to say that we were not the victims of crime in Israel either. One morning, I woke up early in order to catch a flight to Zurich. I walked outside and instead of seeing my car in the driveway, I saw a large empty space. Confused, I tried to recall if I had left my car at a friend and walked home. I called upstairs to Heidi to say that my car had been stolen, and she shouted down to check that hers was still in the garage. I thought that that was incredibly silly thing to ask me until I did look (thinking I would take her car to the airport), and saw that it too was gone. We had been pillaged.

It was then that we noticed a window maneuvered open – the thieves had climbed in and stolen the car keys. They had not taken anything else except the keys and cars, and had even left the cash I had balanced on the top of Heidi's handbag so that I would not be accused of leaving her penniless. It was a sophisticated and well-actioned plan, but none of us were dead. We were enormously grateful.

And then Heidi fell pregnant with our third son. Pregnancy had never been easy for Heidi and this one was going to be no exception. All the challenges of the emigration came to the fore and Heidi battled emotionally. But when we did understand these swings were beyond the norms, we knew that we had little choice but to face it. There were years that were hard and real and there was nowhere to hide. But her journey and the wisdom and strength she has acquired have ultimately given me the ability to let my guard down and be who I am.

Alex was born ill. He had wet-lung syndrome and spent days in intensive care. We were foreigners, and despite the magnificent care, we sorely missed being in our home environment where we owned the system and could navigate the network. When he was ready to be discharged, the CFO of the hospital came to see me and suggested that if I brought cash, then maybe he would "talk a better deal". Coming from a rather straight-laced South Africa, I could never imagine negotiating with a hospital, but hell, this was the Middle East and if they wanted to negotiate, negotiate I would. And I think I got a good deal.

Either way, he got well and we celebrated his circumcision at my in-laws' home and he would turn out to be the easiest of our children – third child and trouble-free motoring. The irony didn't escape us and we struggled as parents to forge an identity for him. The epilepsy that he developed later would make it easier as this became part of his uniqueness – something that we would learn to celebrate as being part of who he is, and not hide it away.

I made lifelong friends in Ra'anana. Ra'anana filled me socially and creatively. I travelled and I socialised, but actually, I was bored.

And I felt disconnected to the world of trade, a world I craved and loved. It was at that time that I attended the FerroAlloys conference in Istanbul, Turkey. The rush I got from those conferences was addictive. I would meet people with multiple opportunities from all over the world, I made lists of options and I forged relationships that would last many years. In Turkey in particular, where there was one kosher restaurant, I banded together a bunch of Jewish guys I had not met before. It included someone from Sweden, the Netherlands, Peru, Spain and a few from New York. A group of young like-minded strangers connected by the industry that we were in and by the need to eat kosher. It was a magical evening, and 18 years later, many of us are still connected and still friends. There was only one person I actually did business with (the quiet Spaniard who didn't care about kosher but somehow joined us anyway), but it was evenings like this that reinforced how lucky we were to be in this industry.

Indeed, commodity traders still ruled the world.

Chapter Nine
GOING GLOBAL

AND THEN I had a conversation with a guy I knew in our neighbourhood. Not someone I was friendly with, but someone who wanted to chat about Alloys. In Israel this was rare; I leapt at the opportunity to do so. We met for coffee and he explained something called "Business to Business". I hadn't heard of it and I didn't like it one bit, but it made sense. Essentially he and a few colleagues wanted to set up a commodity trading hub where buyers and sellers could meet online and trade products. It was clear to me that the Internet was changing the world and that unless the commodity space could redefine itself, it was destined to go the way of the New York trader. Slowly I joined this group of mavericks. Our goal was to create an online market for the physical delivery of commodities. We would create a hub where logistics, services, banks, buyers and sellers could meet, negotiate and conclude, as well as organise the finance and the logistics component of the trade. It was ambitious and it was exhilarating, but it was also unnerving, as it could destabilise a whole industry.

I became CEO and Gerson was COO. We were as different as it was possible to be. It was a partnership that would last for 16 years, where we loved and hated each other. It was one where we respected each other, mostly, but where we were always honest and could trust each other. I was the social one that people were drawn to and the peacemaker. I was softer and more approachable. I was the solution-finder and the compromise-maker. He was the detail-guy, would call it like it is and find holes in any situation. You liked him or you didn't, and many didn't. He was smart and a workaholic. It was a brilliant partnership and also an atrocious one, as we inhabited different stratospheres. We often joked that we stayed together for the sake of the children. We didn't need to define what the children were.

Our strategy was brilliant. Trading companies were lost and seeking their way. We all knew the world was changing, but no one knew where it would go. So, we approached various trading companies – in Europe, the USA, and South Africa and convinced them to come on board. They would bring trade and traction to the site by placing their products on the site and nurturing the sale along the way. In the case of Metalmin, we brought them on board too, and concluded a lot of chrome foundry sales through the site. Most of the real work was done offline but it was a training process. It was also a way to not lose sight of the company I had helped birth. It worked, and I remained connected to it, and to the South African trade environment.

The venture capital funds were throwing money at us and I watched flabbergasted. I was a trader who made his money from watching and maximising every cent. I recall one meeting where we were going through budgets and our funders complained that our "burn rate" wasn't fast enough. This was nonsensical for a trader who was trained to maximise profit by squeezing every cent out of a trade, but I was in their world now and had to play by their rules. They also insisted that I move to New York – the place that was fast becoming the hub for these kinds of companies.

And so we moved. We took offices on 5th Avenue. We hired people, worked closely with our technology developers and followed our strategy. It was a crazy time – company functions were extreme and we attended them with the confidence and arrogance that affirmed we'd be the next big thing. Public listings were happening all around us, no one was profitable and no one seemed to care. I remember having a company get-together at Windows of the World, which was a venue at the top of one of the Twin Towers. We were above the cloud and I stood alone at the window looking down on the city below. It was a surreal moment for me and I remember looking out over the city and wondering how I had arrived at this point and where it would all lead. In retrospect it would become more bizarre, when not only this area of commerce, but the very building where we celebrated its success, would come crashing down.

Revenue streams were debated as concepts akin to a life after death discussion – it would be great to know, but impossible to prove and almost with the same relevance – that we will get there in the end, all will be revealed, so why stress now?

We built a staff, spent hundreds of hours on technology and managed the global aspect of the business. It needed to be global and so our teams travelled to anywhere it was important to be.

It was also a time when moral boundaries became blurred. I was sitting in my office one afternoon and received an email from a guy I didn't know. He explained in some detail that he and his wife wanted to send Michael Greenberg (one of our senior guys), flowers to thank him for something or other. It was meant to be a surprise so if I could provide his home address, but not mention it to Michael, he would be extremely grateful. I had no doubt that the email was written by a woman and screamed for Michael to get into my office.

"What is this and who is she?" I asked. He read the mail and the colour drained from his face. "Shit, shit shit, shit!", he kept repeating and then, realising that I might have divulged his address, said, "You didn't give it to her, did you?" I hadn't and I forced him to sit down and explain what the hell was going on.

Michael was a family man. Married with three children, a religiously-observant man who loved his children almost as much as he loved sex. When we had initially met, and he heard I was South African, he provided me with a list of South African girls he "knew", some of which I now pass on the way to synagogue on a Saturday. Michael had travelled to India for business and had met a lovely Swiss girl at the carousel while collecting his luggage. They clearly hit it off and spent the next few days getting to know each other. There was obviously not much work done.

What it seems he neglected to mention to her was the fact that he was married. And when she found out, she didn't take it that well. In fact, she took it rather badly and decided that it was her duty to inform Michael's wife of his behaviour. This was one Swiss girl who did not remain neutral.

He was in a panic, but even more so, when he realised that everyone in the office had received the same email. This girl was determined.

So we spoke it through and decided that he needed to go home and tell his wife that he had erred. He needed to offer to go for counselling and to make it right. We felt that it was the best approach and the most sensible. He left feeling positive and hopeful. They were divorced six months later.

And then there was Steve, one of our technology guys, who died unexpectedly. He was 30, fit and slim and was a typical "techy". He was a really decent guy from Staten Island, a place that I'd heard of, but had no reason to visit, until now. It was a Jewish holiday and I was at home on Long Island (managing my anxiety), and my phone must have rung 30 times. I knew there was trouble and remained calm until the sun set. Steve had apparently had a heart attack. That was what we were told and there was no way of finding out anything to the contrary. In truth it didn't matter – it was horrible and tragic, either way.

As I was his boss, and I had a British accent, I was asked to speak at his wake. I am convinced that I was asked so as to provide an international feel to the event, and reluctantly accepted. I was not used to this flavour of Jewish burial, where the deceased is dressed in his Sunday finest for us all to see and found myself telling his mother how great he looked in his coffin. As I said it I realised how bizarre it sounded and waited for her to be appalled by my insensitivity, but she seemed to think so too, and explained he hadn't worn that suit since his bar mitzvah. To this I had no idea how to respond so I nodded in a boss sort of way and then mounted the podium to bid farewell to Steve in my most British of all accents (being South African, of course).

We moved to an area of New York known as The Five Towns (of which Woodmere was one), in Long Island. Gerson warned me that it wouldn't be for us and that we would not be happy there. But the schools were excellent, the community cohesive, so we took the decision to move there despite the warnings.

It was death for me. We were attractive as a family. We had cute British accents (being South African, of course), our children had manners, we appeared to have money (the appearance of wealth being all that counted) and we spoke exotically of foreign lands. So, our house was full and we were social, but it didn't feel real to me.

In South Africa and in Israel, the two places we had lived, we had lived amidst adversity. Although protected by the bubbles in which we lived, in both places, one cannot ignore the tragedy of apartheid, the legacy it created and the aftermath of poverty and illness that will last for generations. Every street corner bears testimony to a failed people and unspoken misery, and not to notice or feel, is to have no heart. Israel has its own story of war, of loss and constant terror and threat. Alongside its success is the price paid for its existence. Adversity amongst Jew and Moslem is real, and it is tangible and heartbreaking.

"Tragedy" in The Five Towns is when one receives full-cream milk when one asked for low-fat, or a well-toasted bagel when one asked specifically for "lightly toasted". It creates a different understanding of the world and it is wonderful to live in, but not necessarily good for one's soul. It's like eating sugar, all day every day.

Life in the suburbs was prescribed. You didn't wear a straw hat to synagogue after Labor Day and could certainly not wear white shoes after this milestone. Mrs Five Towns drove a Town and Country and Mr Five Towns drove a Saab, unless it was his "station car" in which case, allowances were made and he could drive something a little shabbier. How long you went to Acapulco for in winter determined what kind of financial year you had, and not having a fur coat for the winter was somewhat of a shame. Most people strained under the financial burden of private education, the right clothes, summer camp and acceptable vacations, but all cracks were quickly covered up by another layer of make-up, so everyone looks gorgeous and smiles a lot. "Fear of not fitting in" is what drove the community and so everyone conformed and no one questioned.

Sundays were suburban hell that included Little League, pizza and then birthday parties. We were not native baseballers, and this was all too apparent to all when I went into the sports store and asked for a bat for my son Ben, who was left-handed. The shop assistant looked at me strangely and asked why he needed to know that, and still not realising my ignorance, I explained that I didn't want to buy a bat for a right-handed kid. As though talking to a non-English speaker he explained loudly and slowly that baseball bats are round and so it really shouldn't make much difference.

Beach clubs, school dinners, Shabbat afternoon clothes all made very little sense to us. (It turns out that children needed formal wear for synagogue and then semi-formal wear for lunch and the afternoon.) It felt like New Yorkers had created a dreaded social order akin to that of their British ancestors, who ironically had literally emigrated to escape the constraints. News was local and dramatic and was constantly "crossing live" to nothing at all. Headlines like "How safe is the food in your neighbourhood supermarket?" screamed at us from our televisions and continued to stimulate fear. I could not access international news on TV, as even the news channels that we had watched outside of America were different. I felt the rest of the world was slowly disappearing and I started to panic.

I often found conversations around our dinner table to be myopic. Fifteen years after leaving The Five Towns I am still shocked that an educated professional guy could ask me whether Black people in South Africa insisted on being called African Americans. I also recall with clarity the look that Heidi gave me across the table that meant "shut the hell up, don't say what you are thinking – we need friends." I did shut up about that, as the glint of his freshly manicured nails caught my attention and I spent a moment pondering what colour he had requested. His wife happened to be a speech therapist in Brooklyn which fascinated me more, and I couldn't help asking her if she was required to teach children to say "dawg" for dog and "cawfee" for coffee? She said yes and looked at me strangely, clearly wondering why I had even asked the question and why someone like Heidi had married someone like me. By then Heidi was a bit of a local hero as she baked "from scratch" and even separated her own egg-whites. There was an audible gasp from the woman when she mentioned this, not realising that Heidi simply didn't know one could actually purchase preseparated ones.

But I am ashamed to say that they did teach me some vital lessons – caffeine and Tylenol suppositories.

As an orthodox Jew we have a few fast days a year that require us to neither eat nor drink for the duration of the fast. Nil per mouth. Some are 12 hours (sunrise to sunset) and some are 25 hours, dusk to sunset the following day. For coffee drinkers, these fasts present a very real challenge. Well, not in The Five Towns where the Friendly Pharmacist has created these magnificent, life-changing pods, well, before Nespresso did. And you don't need a machine, if you understand what I mean. All one does require is a freezer, as these little jewels need to be kept frozen for efficient insertion. It was not uncommon to see people at the Synagogue, or at work on fast days where work was not prohibited, popping out for a quick "coffee". They would return with a glint in the eye rarely seen on such a day. I am not proud of the fact that I fasted very easily that year, but nor am I as ashamed as the people in the neighbourhood who ordered the decaf option.

And then there is summer camp. Parents in this community send their children away to camp for six to eight weeks. Whereas I am comfortable owning the characteristic that I don't particularly like other peoples' children (except a select few), I certainly would expect their own parents to do so.

It was towards the end of a fantastically enlightening meal that this delightful couple also gave us an invaluable tip if we ever decided to abandon our children to teenage counsellors who would, no doubt, be equipped to raise, nurture and love hundreds of children for two months. She told us that the thing to do is to buy the kids 60 new pairs of underwear so that they could wear and chuck (so to speak) every day. This way one could be assured that the children were clean and fresh daily, and didn't have to suffer the indignity of doing their own washing (God forbid) in the magnificently equipped laundry provided by the camp and run by the counsellors. The disposable society was now also starting to focus on our underwear and I knew that there wasn't much more I could handle.

I would have been in great banner-holding company in The Five Towns of Long Island. Interestingly, although I can be a social chameleon, (which is a requirement for a banner-holder), I could never do this in The Five Towns of New York, where so many were doing just that.

Chapter Ten

LIFE AFTER DEATH

AND THEN OCTOBER 2000 changed the landscape. The stock market crashed. Our financiers folded and we were left drifting and confused. Suddenly our burn-rate wasn't impressive and it was clear that the time to answer the "life after death" question had arrived. It was also clear that we had very little time to make that happen. The next few months were a struggle and stressful, but would ultimately teach me many valuable skills. Winter was setting in in New York and it would be harsh. Day after day I took the Long Island Railway into the city, with my newspaper folded in columns so that I could read it without disturbing others. I felt real pity for myself, especially when December arrived and I thought of my family back in South Africa, all on summer vacation in Muizenberg. Day after day, as I boarded the LIR to the City and home, I would think of them going back and forth to the beach. It was the first time in my life I was properly miserable.

The burden of responsibility was immense. We were strangers in a country I didn't understand, the business was clearly a struggle and as money from the Venture Capital Funds began drying up around us, the pressure increased. My family seemed to fit in better than I did, and I could sense a distance growing between us.

My wife spent her days having coffee and shopping, and my children were sounding American. School lunches were pizza and hot dogs, and how many your child would be given was determined at the beginning of the school year. They would watch children's TV programmes and be bombarded by food and toy advertisements at breaks. As a result, they were always hungry or in "desperate need" of the latest plaything.

When Heidi took them out of school one day to take them shoe shopping (apparently "everyone was doing it"), I became increasingly concerned. I really didn't like what we were becoming. And to be clear, I can be as shallow and materialistic as the next guy, but The Five Towns was a whole different level.

By April, the weather hadn't turned. We flew to Israel on a cold and rainy New York day, to meet my family for Passover. We would return to the same weather. In Israel I watched the interaction between my nieces and nephews and their cousins (all of whom still lived in South Africa), as well as their interaction with my parents who were part of their lives. I looked at our three boys, bloated and cumbersome from the pizza lunches, dressed in their dry-clean-only linen outfits, certainly no longer climbing trees. I felt real regret. Regret that I would be as foreign to my children as my European grandparents were to me when they spoke of "home" and of a life they led prior to coming to South Africa. Regret that they were evolving into loud, contrived and ultimately insecure people who needed to be heard in fear that they would not be visible.

I realised then that the only adults involved in our children's lives were their parents. "Intergenerational Day" was a painful reminder of this status. In general, there were no grandparents, no uncles and aunts and no friends who genuinely cared and took the time to ask them a question, or listen to their tales. This is the pain of emigration and one that I could no longer bear. I was sure then that we would leave New York, and that it would indeed be a rough journey for the family, something life in The Five Towns had not equipped them for.

Heidi was by now pregnant with our fourth child and I broke the news to her that I wanted to leave New York. It didn't go well. Our options were to return to Israel and for me to commute to South Africa (assuming that I took control of Metalmin), or go back to South Africa as a family. We had witnessed the strain of the commuting family as my father-in-law still continued to shuttle between the two countries. It was not something to take lightly. On this basis we made the decision to return to South Africa, but it was not an easy one. Heidi felt that returning after being out of the country for five years was a failure and a massive step backwards. I longed for a place where I felt a sense of belonging. My in-laws were desperately against it, having taken the difficult steps many years before, and my parents were supportive. We flew back to South Africa on July 4th 2001. I was resolute and determined. Heidi cried for the entire 18 hours it took SAA to bring us back. Six weeks later the world would shift slightly on its axis when the Twin Towers, the very place we had enjoyed a company function three months before, come crashing down.

We purchased a house in Johannesburg that needed some work, so we stayed with my parents for a few months during this process. Although they took care of us, contained and nurtured and loved us, it was not a happy time for us as a family. Into this, our fourth son was born.

Although I know that Judah was not an easy baby, I don't have any clear memories of him. The first years of his life were the start of our active involvement in Metalmin and when I reflect, it is clear that I was not around for him. Whatever energy I had for the kids was utilised on the older boys and he became Heidi's responsibility and domain. When his learning difficulties became more apparent, I was forced to step in. The one thing I remember was vehemently arguing with his nursery school teacher that he should not have to stay back a year. We debated this incessantly and I simply could not accept my son repeating that year. The teacher claimed that it was a maturity issue and that staying back would help. I refused to listen and he landed up repeating First Grade before being moved to a remedial school. I happened to be right regarding the irrelevance of maturity levels, but I also could not tolerate the embarrassment and discomfort that came with my son repeating a year.

Our most difficult cross-border move by far was the migration back to South Africa. Like many immigrants, we imagined that everything would stay the same after our departure and that those left behind to battle through their daily lives, with an ever-present void created by our decision to leave. We also assumed that other people's children would stay the same size and nothing would have happened that we did not know about. This was obviously not the case. It was slightly shocking to realise that life went on perfectly well without us. No one fell apart and everyone continued as though we had never left. In some ways it's like a slice being taken out of a pie – maybe it is noticed for a while, but when the pie is pushed together, although smaller, it still looks whole. There is also the assumption that as we were not strangers to this environment, that we were self-sufficient. It was immigration without the "newness", and without the sense of adventure.

But it was also nurturing. My family had all remained in South Africa and two of Heidi's sisters had returned when they married South African men. Two more would follow later, but then we were beginning to enjoy what it meant to be back in the bosom of a large family. Our children went to the same school as I did as a child and were amazed by how everyone seemed to know them, their parents, uncles and aunts and grandparents. After a few days Zac asked me if we were famous – and again I realised that taking them abroad had deprived them of the sense of belonging that we had enjoyed growing up. He also asked me why in South Africa we had to sing, "Good morning Mrs Jacobson" whilst standing at their desks. And how it was that teachers could shout at and insult the children, calling them pigs, and no one seemed to mind.

But there was more good than bad, and we found that although the South African schooling system was a lot less exciting, it allowed our children to be young for longer and gave them a better all-round grounding than we had experienced in the other schooling systems.

We had also deprived them of a sense of their own history, and although Israel had given them a National and Jewish context and sense of belonging, New York had not. It was this that we reversed by returning to South Africa. It was a confusing time. I remember walking past the bathroom where our two boys were bathing and talking about sports and overheard Ben (who was five) ask Zac who was seven years old who we "rooted" for. Was it The Yankees or Bafana Bafana? I stopped in my tracks and listened for the answer. I didn't hear him shake his head, but I heard the "Oh Ben!". We had clearly confused them beyond all hope.

Now there were other adults to talk to them and take an interest in their lives. And then, our boys began to climb trees. Wrists would be broken as they dived out of a tree house to escape an "exploding bomb". Teeth would be cracked in a rough game of cricket. Clothes would be torn, and dry-clean-only children's clothes were kept for family weddings. Our children were finally, once again, just children.

Chapter Eleven

TIME CHANGE

BEFORE LEAVING THE USA, I had approached Gerson and asked him what his plans were. He was clear that he intended returning to Israel (and had come to New York on that basis), but was not certain as to what he would do. He was not concerned about the prospect of extensive travel and we both recognised how well we worked together. I made him an offer to join me in Metalmin as an equal partner, and together we would take this small company that had been limping along for some time and do something special with it.

Metalmin in the meantime was a small operation. It employed five people and traded a smattering of products – some ores, but mainly alloys. By way of background, these products are generally used as ingredients for the production of either steel or stainless steel. Chrome ore for example, is mined and then processed into a higher quality ore by removing the waste. It is then either sold as ore or beneficiated further through a smelting process into Ferrochrome. This takes place in massive furnaces where other flux and additives are mixed into the pot. The Ferrochrome is then used to make stainless steel. It is a dull and unsexy industry, but it is the cornerstone of the construction and manufacturing industries, and very often the measure of local economies. In many respects, it's the front line of industry and often the best way to measure the pulse of global trade. On my trips to China (that would later on become frequent), I would try and count the cranes I saw between the airport and the hotel as a measure of growth, as this would have a direct impact on the raw material requirement. In all the years I did this, I never once completed the task, for they were always too numerous. But in 2001 China was only waking up as far as our industry was concerned, and it would take a few years to develop into the hungry beast that would consume everything in its path.

No matter how technology would change this universe, commodity trading required human to human contact. Dr Seuss could well have been thinking of trading when he wrote "Oh the places you'll go! There is fun to be done! There are points to be scored. There are games to be won. And the magical things you can do with that ball will make you the winning-est winner of all." Oh, the places I have been, from Madagascar to Kazakhstan, Czech Republic to Zambia, South of France to Inner Mongolia, Hungary to Mexico and of course all the well-known and well-travelled cities around the world. London, New York, Paris, Monte Carlo, Rome, Athens, Tokyo, Mumbai, New Delhi, Singapore, Port Louis, Zurich. And the people I have met

– presidents of African Nations, financiers and lawyers around the world, thieves and rogues and con men and the artisanal miner who simply wants to mine, sell his product, feed his family and do it all again the next day. The trader is expected to be chameleonic, interested in everything and to be able to adapt with ease to local culture. Holding your business card with two hands in China is a given and knowing how to toast, drink and greet in the local morays are basics of the trade.

Tolerance is critical. I recall a morning in Lusaka where I had scheduled meetings on the hour and a half from 7:30 am. My 7:30 am arrived at 9 am, my 9 am at 12 pm and 10:30 am around 11:30 am. I was exasperated and convinced of an imminent clash of appointments. When I challenged the 9 am guy (at 12 pm) he looked at me and smiled and I knew then that I had failed to appreciate a fundamental of trade in that region. "Sir", he explained, "God might have given White men Watches, but He gave us African men Time." From then on, I realised that if I were to do business in this area, I would give myself an extra day and not try and inflict my self-imposed schedule on potential partners.

Being a real business traveller means that you encounter experiences that bring into sharp focus your life and its smallness. For instance, the absolute certainty you feel that you are going to die on an Indian road; it is the loneliness of a text sent home, saying your life is going to end shortly, as cars, trucks, tuk-tuks and pedestrians come at you from all sides; it is the desperation of an SOS transmitted that you do not want to be buried in India. It is the appreciation of a clean toilet when you have an upset stomach on the road between Delhi and Agra. You don't know serenity, beauty and charm until you have returned to India for the second time, with your senses prepared for the onslaught. You haven't travelled for business if you haven't battled to breathe in Beijing, or longed to see the sky that is obscured by pollution, or until you have Sprüngli chocolates and a double macchiato for dinner in Zurich Airport. You are not a traveller until you are recognised by flight attendants, as well as fellow migrants, as a familiar face.

You haven't travelled as a married man until you have learned that no matter how much fun you have, the response to "how was your evening?" is, in sullen-teenager speak, "fine". I made that mistake when I was just a youngster. I had meetings in London for the whole day and was really tired in the evening. A friend had asked me out for dinner but I just didn't feel like going. I spoke to Heidi on the phone after my day and she convinced me to go out and enjoy myself and in fact, live a little. So I got dressed and went downstairs to the lobby to wait for my friend.

On the spur of the moment, I took a ticket from the concierge for a new show called Mamma Mia that had just come to the West End. So, I went out for dinner, shared a bottle of wine, and when he went home, I went to the show which I really loved. It was a wonderful evening. The following evening when Heidi asked, and I replied "I had the best time last night", it wasn't as well received as I had anticipated. Apparently being able to have the "best evening" without her was not something that we valued in our marriage. So, I never did again. All other evenings were just fine. From then on, the base-line was "miserable" and

I peaked at "fine".

I also discovered that Heidi was very little help with decision making. I was on a Virgin flight from London to Johannesburg and was flying Upper Class. Whilst the flight was filling up, the flight attendants handed out request cards where you could tick your preference for a head and neck massage, manicure, pedicure and a few other options. I couldn't decide and before switch off I called Heidi to assist with this decision. It was around 6 pm back home and while I do appreciate that Heidi had her hands full with our three boisterous young boys needing to bath, eat and get put to bed, her attitude was not what I had expected and I was forced to make the decision completely on my own. I didn't even know she could curse like that!

My two worlds would sometimes collide – the extent of this clash became glaringly obvious on one of my first trips to Korea, where I was meeting a Chrome Sand customer. He was enormously hospitable and arranged a private dinner for us. This was standard in many places, but I was ill-prepared. I had a junior colleague with me and on entering the private room we were confronted with a line of magnificent women. My host explained that I was to have first choice of hostess for the evening and that I should do so forthwith. Sensory overload. I had clearly not anticipated this. I was young, a little naïve, definitely unprepared. I had not thought this through as I liked to do, ahead of time. And each of the hostesses was more beautiful than the next (not sure if I mentioned that). Concerns of betraying Heidi; intellectual issues of objectifying women as they stood patiently waiting to be chosen for the evening; fear of losing the customer if I insulted my host, and mostly, would I be able to decline before real damage was done to my moral integrity. All this crashed around in my head as I calmly selected my stunning hostess for the evening.

My chosen hostess went to work immediately, loosening my tie and undoing the top button of my shirt, and slipping her hand inside, dispelling any doubt as to what her objective was for the evening, pouring me a drink and hanging onto every word I said (not that she spoke enough English to do any such thing). But the dinner was about business and so we made toasts to long-term business, to real business friendships and to growing this segment of the market, container by container, and to the future. We spoke about chrome sand quality and how this could be improved, all whist the alcohol flowed and I became more and more unhinged. It also needs to be noted that I am kosher observant, which means that I am very limited in what I can eat at these dinners and would usually stick with vegetables to be certain. This is not advised when consuming large amounts of alcohol. In addition, I was not much of a drinker in my youth and was always the designated driver, so I really had very little muscle memory for consumption of this kind. At some point I knew that I needed to step out of it all in order to regain some perspective and did so by taking a much needed bathroom break. Bathroom breaks would eventually become one of my strategies, along with an important call I would have to place or receive (after sending a text for someone to call me), to pull back, think about what was going on, and then head back in. I called Heidi from the men's room and was relieved that she found my predicament amusing. Well, I think she did, as she was laughing so much I'm not really sure what she said.

I went back to the dinner clear-headed and resolved. When my hostess's hands found their way back inside my shirt, I gently pointed to my wedding ring (one item that Ben had not yet flushed down the toilet), indicating by this gesture, that although this was all very well and good, and that she most likely was a lovely person, her hands should drift no further. Apparently it was not as clear to her as it was to me, and her face lit up as she squealed, "Oh, you want me to be your wife tonight?" Well, no, actually I didn't.

And herein lay the problem. My business objective was to forge a stronger relationship with my customer. Her objective was to end the evening back in my hotel room. That simply was not going to happen. I tried whatever I could to divert her trajectory, until I had no choice (or so I thought), but to speak directly to my host and explain that although I greatly appreciated his hospitality, this was not something that I was comfortable with. It was a mess. He was deeply offended that I rejected his Korean hospitality and culture and I, in turn was offended that he refused to respect mine. When I climbed into my taxi – alone – we agreed that the evening was superb and that we had had a wonderful time, and that all was marvellous. We never did business again.

The very real high that I got from travelling was addictive. If I didn't travel for a few weeks, I started to feel constrained by my environment and everything around me. It got to the point where I could only appreciate what we had by seeing it from afar and I noticed it became a trend, even within my own family. I would often find myself, say on the beach when holidaying, stepping back and looking at Heidi and the children playing, and enjoying this more than actually being part of the game. I loved meeting people on planes, on trains and in meetings. If I had to be away for the weekend (something I avoided), I would find a synagogue and a Shabbat meal where I knew that other businessmen from around the world congregated and I'd make connections across the globe. I made good friends in so many cities around the world and tried to coordinate a dinner or drinks wherever our paths crossed. It educated and enlightened me and I felt like I was truly a citizen of the world.

And then there is the dark side of travel. It's the part that deprives you of your children's school concerts, sports games and parent-teacher feedback. It's the part that forces your spouse to act as a single parent for a time and then to be questioned for the choices you weren't there to make together. It's the part that takes you out of the rhythm of the family and a few days to get back into it after your return. It's the part that allows you not to have to resolve an issue as it will most likely be forgotten by your return. It forces your wife to learn to live without you and gives you a life that your family cannot understand or relate to.

I loved the travel, but hated the going. I felt torn by my leaving and would need to find something to look forward to on each trip. I would promise myself a walk along the Bahnhofstrasse, a coffee at an outdoor café, a visit to a museum, a show, or purchase of a much-coveted item. I had a very specific process that I would go through to get ready for a trip. I needed exactly an hour to pack, shave, shower, check the necessary – travel documents, credit cards, cash, chargers and business cards – to walk out the door into the waiting car that the airline would send for me. Each step helped me burrow deeper into myself and by the time I walked out the door I was stressed about the trip ahead, but gave no voice to the pain of leaving. I taught myself to bury the feelings that I might have and as a result, became an expert at not feeling and not recognising my own emotions, until impossible to contain.

The hardest part was the drive to the airport, and I could not relax even in the lounge after a whisky, where I would nod to fellow frequent travellers and share a look that said everything but nothing. I would check that everyone had settled at home, which by now they would have done, do a rotation around the airport, buy magazines I would never read, board through the business line, and then settle myself into 1A. One more check on the family and a "Switching off, love you" WhatsApp would announce that I am now out of contact, as the plane taxied to transport us to another world.

The places I visited educated and astounded me. Whether I loved or hated them, whether I wanted to return or never set foot there again, they enriched and entertained. They filled a part of me I couldn't access in Suburban Anywhere.

Sometimes a trip simply would not go well. One such trip was a conference that we were attending in Kazakhstan. It was a fascinating place to visit and I arrived a day before the conference for various logistical reasons. I spent the day trying to get a sense of the place. Gerson was to arrive the next day. At 6 am my phone rang and I could see it was him. The time change was about four hours so this meant it was really 2 am for me. I was not impressed that he felt the need to call me to announce his arrival, but nevertheless, I answered groggily and could immediately hear the panic in his voice.

"Howard, get hold of the conference organisers. I am in trouble."

Gerson was not a chance-taker, so this made little sense. Fully awake and in problem solving mode, I asked him what was going on.

"I got to passport control and they asked me for my visa. I showed them the page and they said, 'no, where is your visa?' I said it was there and they showed me that my visa is for Uzbekistan and not Kazakhstan!"

Apparently this is not a mistake that the Kazaks take lightly (I have no idea what the Uzbeks would think of it).

"They are deporting me in the next half hour unless I do something! Get hold of the organisers at the hotel and see if they can help!"

Well they didn't help. And Gerson was deported back to Moscow, where his passport was returned after he had been bundled back onto another plane for home.

Later that trip I received a call that my sister-in-law (my older brother's wife) had had a serious stroke and I would need to come home. Getting out of Kazakhstan is not as easy as one might think, and I only managed to get back 48 hours later, by which time, to my irritation, the crisis was over.

Madagascar is a world of its own. Less than a three-hour flight from Johannesburg, it somehow manages to straddle various continents. It is African, Indian and French all at once, and is one of the most disappointing places I have been to. I had long had a romantic notion of this massive island and I am told that you cannot judge it by its capital, Antananarivo, the only place I have been.

What I saw was a filthy, overcrowded, polluted, poverty stricken ramshackle town that bore no resemblance to the vision that I had. The hour's drive from the airport was in a non-airconditioned car sans suspension. There are no highways, so the drive is a stop-start affair, most of the way being crowded with people, shops, food, fresh and cooked, and smoke. Because the car windows need to be open and people are continually walking past the car, I always felt exposed and anxious until I reached the hotel. The stagnant bodies of water, the rice paddies and shanties, all contributed to the feeling that everything was out of control.

The drive invariably made me nauseous and by the time I arrived at my destination I would be gasping for air and trying not to throw up on the steps of the hotel as the locals rushed to assist in carrying my bag and asked for hand-outs. I learnt to bring chewing gum as that sometimes helped.

That is until you meet the President. The contrast between the street outside and the grounds of his palace takes your breath away. The serenity is more pronounced by the knowledge of the chaos outside the walls.

His palace is beautifully appointed, orderly and quiet, as is he.

On our first meeting with him, I was taken aback by his youthful looks and energetic approach. It was hard to believe that this man had staged a coup d'état and was shunned by the world. He gave Gerson and me significantly more time than we were allocated and we left our first meeting enthralled and inspired. He offered his support and gave us assurances that we would work together as partners in order to achieve the best return for his country and to achieve maximum efficiencies and values for his precious resource.

But his chain of command was as polluted as the environment and dealing with his appointee was not so simple.

Her office was situated in a busy street of Tana, not far from the palace and I visited her on at least four occasions. The building was run down and dark and after climbing the stairs to the floor where her office was, we were greeted curtly and told to wait.

She always made me sit in a small windowless anteroom while she completed whatever it was that she was very busy with. I was offered no refreshments by her reception despite the heat and lack of air.

After waiting the required twenty minutes, I'd be called in to her office. It would take a few seconds for my eyes to adjust to the bright light that bathed her space. Her office was enormous and decorated with care. It had gleaming wooden floors, a lounge area with leather couches and a sparkling Espresso machine at the far end.

She never learned my name and never could quite place which

company I represented, despite the fact that she only sold one parcel per quarter, and that we would take at least two out of the four per year traded. She also never offered me coffee, or even a glass of water, despite being fully aware that I had travelled a great distance to meet her. I knew for a fact that she did not entertain many foreign buyers and yet showed no hospitality or interest. She also did not enjoy receiving calls from us and would tell my guys to "stop calling me", when we were trying to close a parcel. She was singularly one of the most unpleasant people I have had to deal with and one of the few in the industry with whom I could not form any connection.

During this time I also got to meet their Minister of Finance who would win the next election and become President. We had breakfast in a beautiful Art Deco Hotel in Paris, just off the Champs Élysées and across the road from Louis Vuitton, and was impressed by his humility and genuine concern for the welfare of his struggling homeland.

Zimbabwe, of course, is an entirely different matter and the truth is that it was a very enjoyable place to visit. I always found people to be welcoming and I've never had a bad travel experience there.

We did have a really bad business experience where we were caught on the wrong side of the chrome ore export ban after we had prefunded product on the ground that we could not move, causing us to lose millions of US Dollars. But the travel aspect was never a difficult one for me.

One of our employees did have a tough time on one of his trips where he was caught taking a 500g sample of chrome ore out the country without a permit. He had simply wanted to have the quality of the sample analysed at a South African laboratory for good order sake and so that we could complete a transaction of significant tonnages. He was stopped at the airport, arrested, and held for two days, then taken to court where he was fined USD25 for his crime. Despite his protestations that he was untouched by the experience, I don't believe that he ever travelled there again.

Chapter Twelve
TELEPHONE CALLS

AND OF COURSE there are the conferences. These working, networking, observing, drinking-fuelled gatherings are the invisible threads that knit the industry together. At any given conference, the question asked is who is going to the next conference in Hong Kong or Berlin or Beijing? The papers are the same, the speakers are repetitive, everyone is afraid to discuss pricing in fear of being called to task, but everyone is there. It is important to be seen and to project the theme of the day. If everyone is finding the market tough, then so do you. If the year has been positive, then yours needed to be even more so. And so it goes. Everyone observes who is spending time with who in order to anticipate the "next big thing". Extramarital affairs are enjoyed and denied, call girls used and discarded and on many an occasion when leaving for an early flight, the elevator stopped at a descending floor to pick up and spew out a tired looking local, teetering on her high heels, on her way home.

As was my role, I often found myself protecting those around me. At one Metal Bulletin Conference in Hong Kong, a standard feature of the trading year, many from the industry gathered at the hotel bar. There was the usual banter, jostling and laughs, but there was also a vibe that felt edgy to me. I could not identify it and continued to enjoy the single malts and cigars being offered and bought. Then as always, someone suggested we move on to somewhere more fun. And somewhere more fun, in Hong Kong, was a club called Sticky Fingers (no kidding) a few blocks away. There were about 30 of us, and no one wanted to seem to be weak, so we all traipsed down the road to the "real fun".

There are relatively few women active in this industry and at conferences, and the ones that are, I believe are in an invidious position. They are generally either accused of "sleeping their way" to success (and to be honest, a few have), or being "tough bitches", or not being strong enough for the industry. None of these accusations are levelled at men. On some level this is a universal challenge for women in the work place, and it does seem more acute in this industry.

That said, there were a few women who were at the conference and with whom I am friendly. Somehow that night I was more concerned than I was normally. So we went to Sticky Fingers and I was watchful as the evening became more and more raucous and more and more out of control. As more alcohol was pushed, the less I drank and the more hyper-vigilant I became. It was clear that something was up. It was now 2:30 am and I had had enough. Not wanting to shirk the responsibility I felt, I tried to convince one of the women to leave, too, and offered to walk her back to the hotel. She was by now enjoying the effects of the alcohol and didn't want to leave which was a concern, but I didn't want to make an issue of it. That said, I signalled an employee who was at the conference with me and who I trusted, and gave him the responsibility of getting her back to the hotel and to her room.

And how right I was. Drinks had been spiked, and the situation grave. An hour later, Larry, my trusted appointee had an extremely hard time wresting her away from one of the guys we suspected did the spiking. Larry is not a small guy and his first team rugby build no doubt played a role in his success. He succeeded, and made sure that she entered her room alone. When we met for lunch the following day, she had no recollection of the evening, or of getting to her room and had no doubt that she had been drugged. To this day she has no idea if the goal was sexual only, or if there was another commercially-related reason that she was targeted.

"The fear of missing out" on one of these conferences is what drives many to attend. Everyone accepts that the price is too high, that it is not worth the time, but still they go. You need to be there to hold up the banner and to say everything that everyone is saying.

Just over two years ago, I was in my office and received a call from my mother. Although I don't answer all of her calls, we have reached an agreement, which came about a few months before this. I was in a meeting with my banks in the boardroom, and my phone rang. It was my mom. I hit silent, but she called again and again and again.

By the sixth call, I could not contain my irritation, asked the banks to excuse me for answering my phone in a meeting, picked it up and said, "Someone had better have died."

Silence. It turned out that my mother was most offended by my answer. According to her, I was not raised to talk that way. It was a shame on me for doing so, and the hurt that I caused was apparently massive. She couldn't imagine what a poor mother she must have been for this to happen. It was her fault, she knew, for not having taught me decency and manners, but, supposedly it wasn't important that she wanted to drop off freshly-made soles for dinner. So, we made a deal later that day (when she stopped sobbing), that if she needed me she would call three times (twice didn't make sense as she needed to call at least twice to make sure that I noticed). And I would answer.

And so, when my phone rang three times that afternoon, I knew I needed to pick up. "Jacqui has had a seizure and is not breathing. Go to the house now," she ordered. Jacqui, 38, married to my younger brother had had medical issues as a result of brain surgery years before. As a result, I never knew whether my presence would be an imposition or a help.

I took the decision to be there, and arrived at the house to find multiple responders still busy with her. My brother, his face ashen with shock, was pacing up and down not sure what to do. My older sister wore a look that told me this was not looking positive. They were fortunate to have two doctors in the complex, both of whom were in the room with the emergency services, all trying their best. It was 40 minutes later, with no progress. Then my father arrived. He had aged on the 20-minute drive from his factory. I asked my mother to take him to the neighbour and stay there with him. I needed him out the way.

I then called one of the doctors out of the room, and asked her to level with me. It was clear that there was no hope – they had been working for way too long. I went to find my brother, gently told him to take his prayer book and to go into the room, and say the Prayer for the Dying for his young wife.

I stood outside the room with my sister, waiting to see if I was needed. I listened to his wracked sobs as he said his prayers, as well as his farewell. It was unquestionably the most painful thing I have ever listened to. Time of death was called a few minutes later. She had left a bereft husband, a little boy of nine and a little girl of four. They were happily playing at friends and had no idea that their mom was dead. I drove him to the funeral the next day and will never forget his words. "I am living everyone's biggest nightmare."

I was meant to leave for Beijing the next night. I am ashamed that it was not a given that I would cancel. I had a conference I needed to go to.

I didn't cancel. I postponed my trip until a few days later where I managed to connect via Europe. During those few days I managed the situation to the best of my ability. The four days I was there passed in a haze and it was then that I heard someone remark, "Every family should have a Howard." I ignored it but felt buoyed by the fact that I was being supportive. It would not take long for that comment to stick in my throat.

I didn't allow myself to grieve for the loss of this young woman, wife and mother. I was all action and all support. My son Ben called me on it, and asked why I hadn't cried like everyone else. I explained that I had no problem with crying, and in fact I had cried, but it was not the truth. I felt my brother's pain acutely and was heartbroken for my nephew and niece, but I didn't internalise, and I didn't pause. That Saturday night I left for Beijing.

I have no recollection of the conference I needed so desperately to be at.

Chapter Thirteen

THE MAGIC OF METAL

INITIALLY THE WAY that we divided the business was for Gerson to manage the marketing and sales, and for me to manage the procurement and logistics. We traded various FerroAlloys and ores but the business was small and needed to have growth focus. The business we were doing was simply unsatisfying.

At this stage, China was an importer of Ferrochrome that they purchased from various regions. South Africa sits with around 70 per cent of the world's chrome reserves and as the demand for stainless steel increased in China, so it started to look at the option of smelting ore themselves to manufacture Ferrochrome, one of the primary ingredients for stainless steel. And where better to look than South Africa?

Initially the volumes were small, freight to China being expensive and the Chinese still skeptical about the quality of the South

African material, as it was inferior to the Indian and Turkish material.

Traditionally these ores were shipped loose in the hold of vessels primarily as a consequence of the volumes. But chrome is a low value product and the bulk shipping costs at that stage often rendered the potential sale unviable. If we wanted this to be a business we knew that we needed to find an angle.

We started to work with various mines and suppliers but it was clear that unless we solved the logistics challenge, we would never be able to compete in China with higher grade ore from other regions.

It was during this time that we noticed through our contacts at the shipping lines, that there was a container imbalance. South Africa was a net importer of finished goods in containers from China, but there was little moving back in containers in that direction. In order to take advantage of this, we struck a deal with the shipping lines, agreeing to pay a small amount and would pack the maximum amount of chrome into a container (unfortunately only 26.5 metric tons) and reposition them back to China. This was a turning point – it was now possible to export material to China at reasonable costs.

It was a brilliant concept and it would change the face of our business and in fact the entire industry.

But it also meant a complete break from tradition. The conventional method was for mines to rail the product to the port where it would be loaded onto vessels either by belts or skips.

Containers on the other hand were packed in warehouses and had to be trucked or railed to the container terminal or depot where it would be loaded along with other containers from that line on to a dedicated vessel.

Very few warehouses had the capability of moving tonnages designed for bulk vessels and so this area also needed to be a focus. There were a number of warehouses in the industry that we were working with on smaller high value products and they were our first option. One particular group had a visionary at its helm and we spent countless hours trying to work out the logistics of this operation. Mark was quirky and different, but he had the sense to know that if he could figure out the way to manage the volumes of chrome coming into his warehouse, and find a way to reposition so many containers, it would place his business in a different realm.

It was not simple at all as material would be trucked in daily in 30 metric ton lots. They would be carrying different grades from different mines and the option of a truck dumping its load on the wrong stockpile could have catastrophic consequences as it could contaminate and affect grades. Material was also being packed and moved on a constant basis so inventory control was critical. It was clear that they would need to invest in capital in order to ensure that they could provide the service.

I recall so clearly the day he got the go ahead from his Board to invest the capital required and to aggressively work with us in this endeavor. I was walking out of our building to go to an unrelated meeting when Mark came running towards me. As he got close to me, I stretched out my hand to shake his, but he ignored it and fell onto his knees in front of me, placed his forehead on the ground in submission and in a bow, repeating "Thank you, thank you!" How does one not feel a little god-like?

Of course time doesn't freeze, and some years later he and his company made the unfortunate decision to enter the trading arena themselves, creating a massive conflict of interest. We had to pull all our tonnage from them and following a rather uncomfortable legal to and fro, they exited the trading side of their business, having done tremendous damage to the integrity of their core focus. He still doesn't take my hand when I extend mine, nor does he prostrate himself before me either.

We moved various tranches of higher grade metallurgical ore until China became used to, and dependent on South African material. It was also at this time that we started to look closely at the platinum industry and its access to chrome ore.

The UG2 reef is one where both platinum and chrome are found. The platinum producers extract the valuable product and traditionally condemned the chrome to waste in the process. As chrome became more interesting however, they started to look at the possibility of extracting the chrome in the slimes and producing the saleable product. The issues are that the material is very fine, considering the platinum extraction process and the chrome to iron ratio is very low, making this difficult for alloy production.

We took a decision to try and move this product into China. Our early success in doing so opened up a whole new sector and assisted in sustaining an industry that was going through tremendous pain. Initially customers were very skeptical and we had to move the product in paper bags which were then placed in large containers (as opposed to packing the material loose) for their trials. But once it became a product that was useable, it provided us with the tonnage and stability that we had long sought.

At our peak, we moved around 120,000 metric tons of chrome ore a month in containers to China. At 26.5 metric per container, this meant packing close to 5000 containers each month. As a result we created congestion at the ports, and we had to start spreading this volume through the various ports in South Africa. The railways were also not functioning efficiently which meant that this tonnage had to be trucked to the warehouses and ports, and with around 30 mt per load. This too became a massive logistical operation. Between on time payments, inland logistics, packing of containers, ocean freight, quality control, the business became a massive logistical operation. Of the 50 people in the office in Johannesburg, most dealt with the movement of the product from mine to market.

I loved building the team. I could tell within three minutes of an interview if the person was appropriate for us or not. I could never really identify what it was that made me think so, and unlike other companies, I didn't have a formula that I employed in the interview. I simply chatted, and found that people reveal more in a conversation than they do when asked questions that they have prepared. Mostly I looked for passion, positive energy and the drive to succeed. I was good at it. Of course I made mistakes, one or two had major significance, but the rest were inconsequential and it either worked or it didn't. We had a very low staff turnover for some years and almost no one left us by choice. Most of our staff was "home grown" in the sense that our business was unique and industry knowledge not easily found. We nurtured, taught and built people. A strong, driven and focused team was formed. The atmosphere was festive and proud. We became the company in the industry that everyone admired and wanted to work for.

It's never as simple as that and we had some notable moments. One night at around 8 pm I received an email that contained an instant message chat between two employees in accounts. The conversation dealt with various issues, but also had some personal views of other members of staff who sat alongside them. And then came another and then another. I started to panic as we had clearly been hacked. I lived around ten minutes from the office and knew I had to get there to see what was going on. On the way I called the Head of Operations and Gerson only to find out that they too were receiving these mails. It was clear that it was being distributed to everyone in the group and that the contents were going to wreak havoc. By 9 pm the office was full and we had shut the server down. China, India and all other offices had also been recipients but because they were ahead we could delete the mails before they woke up.

However in South Africa we had a problem. There was no doubt that everyone would be reading what others had said about them and this could rip the atmosphere apart. The key question was who could do this, and why?

Roy was a very quiet, introverted member of the accounts team. He was painfully thin (not something I admire too much in a person), and very anxious. He also was the only one whose private chats had not been broadcast so that made it, well, glaringly obvious. Not that smart, Roy. So when he came into work the next day, he and I went for a walk that ended with only one of us returning to the office. Truth is I felt desperately sorry for him as he clearly felt excluded from the rather rambunctious team and I guess I was also grateful that he didn't choose other more violent ways of asserting himself – which in South Africa is not a given. This was his way of "going postal", and I guess we needed to appreciate that.

We moved swiftly to control the damage. Although I requested that people didn't open the emails, I could not ensure that they wouldn't. I have no doubt that they read every word.

The people on my South African staff were like my children. When Heidi and I went away, she clung to our offspring as though she would never see them again. I was the same when I travelled on business and I said goodbye to my staff. I begged them not to fight and to try and "be big", knowing full well that by the time I got to the airport, Liran and Farah would be screaming at each other over a payment that he wanted to make to a supplier who Farah knew would never deliver on time.

I loved my staff and I managed them closely and with care. I counselled, I guided and nurtured. And they returned what I gave with their devotion and loyalty. I honestly believed and still believe that I could count on them for anything and that we had a bond that transcended the standard corporate hierarchy. There was respect and commitment and we were family.

We had year-end functions that had everyone marauding through the streets of Johannesburg in Amazing Races that included our suppliers who became part of the game and who absorbed our enthusiasm. We had a Murder Mysteries day that had them negotiating for clues with dubious characters in seedy bars in downtown Johannesburg and in Master Chef Bake-Offs. We had a mock wedding simply because we had never had one, along with a bridal party, formal reception and speeches. We were a little weird but we loved it. We had Whisky Thursdays and we celebrated Spring day, Halloween, Valentine's and every other day we could, along with the decorations and food that related to those days. We worked and we celebrated. We were Jews and Christians and Moslems and Hindus, we were White and Black and Coloured and Indian, and we were an example of how a common goal and mutual respect eliminates differences. The work got done, and commitment unparalleled. I would get to the office at 6:30 am and would not be the first person there – it was where everyone wanted to be. We had a positive energy that attracted and inspired.

We knew what we had was special. We had taken a piece of metal and given it a soul. It was magic.

On the sales side, Gerson developed relationships in China and India and slowly built what was to become a vibrant, committed and well-respected sales channel. He learned and understood the culture and was a natural at it. The interesting aspect to me was that although I was dubbed the "people person", Gerson, with his rough-around-the-edges approach, was respected and loved in the region.

I will never forget a dinner meeting in Dalian, China, where a customer was telling us about pricing and costs which was not consistent with other information we had. It just didn't tally. We were sitting, as was tradition at a round table with Gerson on my right and I quietly whispered, "Gerson, I can't make sense of this pricing. What am I missing?" With that he turned to the table and in his loudest New York voice said, "Howard, of course the pricing doesn't make sense … they are lying to us!" I was mortified. If I suggested one of our suppliers were dishonest on any basis (even though many were), it would destroy the relationship. I waited for the explosion. And then it came … raucous laughter and multiple toasts to Gerson, to Metalmin and to best friends. This was a different world.

Gerson had also formed a particular bond with one of our customers who was the head of procurement at a major state owned company. He came from an elite and respected family, but was a humble and wise person. He and Gerson developed a relationship that became a real friendship and something of value. He joined us and drove the China expansion.

China was the only place where you could get drunk at your 11 am meeting. It is the only place where a "massage" and a "massage" meant two different things depending on the facial expression. It is a place of magnificent hospitality, of immense discipline and faith in leadership.

It was unfathomable to me in many ways. As a Westerner with five children, the subject of the single-child family was obviously of interest. At a dinner with Team China, I once asked some of our staff what would happen if they wanted to have more than one child. I will never forget Tracy slowly and patiently explaining that in China they are only allowed to have one child. I said that I understood that but "I am asking what would happen if you *wanted* to have another?" She looked at me and again explained. "In China we are only allowed to have one child. It is the law." The concept of "want" and "law" was absolutely indistinguishable.

I also found the concept of religion very difficult to explain in China. Although there is a tremendous amount of tradition and traditional days, as much as I tried to understand the meaning and history behind the days, I found the explanations of whomever I asked, to be limited and shallow. This might well be a reflection on the person I asked, or the fact that they considered me incapable of grasping the full meaning, but after many years of travelling to the region, I don't have a grasp of much of the culture and its meaning.

After China was established, India, Mauritius, Zimbabwe, United Kingdom followed. We were finally global, and we were a success.

Chapter Fourteen

THE SHADOW WITH A FAMILY

THE DRIVE TO succeed is borne of different things. For some people, it is hunger. For some, the shame of not having, or the fear of becoming one's parents, who struggle to keep afloat while slowly being eroded in the process. It was different for me. We were financially comfortable and secure. Although there was a bit of juggling, we never really felt a lack. I had no need to amass money, as did some of my counterparts. In fact, I had little interest in the dollars and cents, and was often bothered by all this "money-making". Although I enjoyed the trappings that came with material success, I consoled myself with the notion that I enjoyed building and creating and that this was my real motivator.

But it was simply not true. And it took the violence and the affront to my mortality, along with significant introspection, to realise this. The answer ran a lot deeper than that, and one that I had to face.

I was seeking to fill the one void I felt in my childhood. I desperately craved the recognition I had never felt. I needed to be visible. I needed to be seen. And through my success, I had found the perfect way to achieve that. With success came visibility. I was finally being noticed and getting what I had missed.

I held my banner with pride and it felt good. The more I succeeded the more I needed to. My drug was not the narcotic kind. It was not alcohol or power or control. It was not sex or gambling. It was very simply the external, indisputable and undeniable proof that I was someone to be proud of. I might have been embarrassed when Mark fell to his knees before me, but it was my first taste of a drug that I would become dependent on.

I was slowly and steadily building my own Tower of Babel. I was entering the dangerous realm of the gods, and the view was spectacular.

The journey upward is an exciting and joyful one. The first time you travel business class, the first time that you are met at the door of the plane as a VIP, the first time you are taken through a separate line of passport control is special and privileged. But then it simply becomes the way that you do things and no further thought is given until you need to sit at the back of the plane or stand in line with other travellers. The only way to keep that joy alive is to keep climbing until the ground is so far beneath you, that it is difficult to make out the faces below.

Heidi and I had agreed that in order to keep our children "real" they would not travel in the front of the plane. This was harder for me than was reasonable and so, when it came to travelling with the family, I would find a business related reason to ensure I would have to meet them at our destination. So painful and humiliating was the thought of travelling in economy.

When Alex and I went on a bar mitzvah father-and-son tour to Israel along with five of our friends and their sons, I travelled in business class and Alex in economy. I was the only one not sitting with my son but we were both used to it and it wasn't an issue for either of us.

We stayed at a hotel that was a compromise for me – I couldn't impose my "standards" on others. The room was brown and dark, and looked out onto a wall. I woke up three hours before Alex to deal with my emails, so that the day would be relatively free of work, but of course this was never the case. I consoled myself that I was no different to one of the fathers in Comrades Marathon training mode who woke up two hours early to go running, or the other father who fought with his son like two siblings throughout the tour. But I wasn't like them. I was distracted and stressed, and it was not fair on either of us.

Sharp perspective dawned on me when we took the boys to visit the Singer family, who had lost a son in the Lebanon war. We sat in their living room and they told us the story of their loss, their pain and their pride. His name was also Alex.

As the tour progressed, so I began to see and appreciate the value. I stopped noticing the dull brown room, and rather saw the special time the boys were having running through the hotel in an imaginary war. I began to relax with my friends.

On the way home to South Africa, I still sat in business and Alex in economy, but this time I couldn't get comfortable in my seat.

The vacations that we took with the family were privileged, but limited by connectivity and time out of the office. I accompanied my loved ones to various parts of South Africa, to Chobe in Zambia and to the Victoria Falls in Zimbabwe. We travelled to Russia and the Baltics, to the Mediterranean and to many countries in Europe. We went to Mauritius and London and Israel repeatedly. Through them all, I worked. And I worked and I worked. I stood on the beach and watched them play while I solved a problem in the office. I sent the family on the London's Red Bus tour whilst I crisis-managed across the sea. I met them at restaurants and then stood outside on the phone. I left each holiday early to fly via somewhere else. I answered emails on tours and searched for signals on safari. I balanced carefully on platforms and rocky outcrops where I could muster a cellphone connection and counted the hours when the vessel we were cruising on would still be out of contact range.

I was the shadow that travelled alongside my family with my credit card exposed; making sure that every need was catered for, aside from the one that really mattered.

I bought my glasses in Paris, and I had a watch guy in Zurich. I had stores in London for my shirts and shops for my shoes and I knew where to buy Heidi and the kids what they wanted. I compensated fantastically and returned home bearing gifts so as to divert everyone from the fact that I had not been present.

We bought and decorated homes with no constraints. We spoke about the day I wouldn't work so hard, and we would be able to enjoy the one commodity that we couldn't purchase. Time.

Today I am enormously critical of what I had become, but I have to acknowledge that this is not the full picture of who I was. I remained essentially a person who wanted to fix the world. I knew that one way to do this was with money. I don't believe that I gave to causes to increase my social profile, but was often taken advantage of in this area.

I was an easy target for any charity. Maybe out of some form of guilt about what I had been blessed with, or maybe out of my need to create myself into what I perceived myself to be, it became harder to turn people away. I began to feel abused by the system that I had happily become part of. Donor fatigue began to take hold and I avoided rather than confronted those that I was not happy to meet.

There is an uneasy relationship between the giver and the receiver, and I could never find my place in this system. I couldn't determine who my friends were and when I was "the target", because my reality dictated that everyone was a friend. When on a few occasions it did become clear that I was "being played", I reacted dramatically. There was no room in my construct for this two-facedness.

On one occasion, I was asked to meet with the fundraiser of an educational college who was visiting from abroad. We met at my office where he presented me with a bottle of Johnny Walker Blue Label whisky. This clearly established what his expectations were, and it annoyed me tremendously. I did not want gifts from the people to whom I was donating. It made no sense to me at all. It was apparent from the first meeting that we would not see eye-to-eye as there was no way that I could be comfortable with where the money would be going. I did not meet him again and he later sent me a cryptic text that read "Dear Howard, they asked Al Capone why he robs banks. He answered, 'because they keep the money there'. I am running after you because you know what institutions mean and have the track record to prove it. Please find five minutes to meet me." I didn't respond or ask for clarity, so I never found out whether I was being compared to Al Capone or a bank who was being robbed.

I also tested the recipients a bit. If I didn't get feedback from an institution that I was donating to on a monthly basis, I would stop my donation for a few months to see how long it would take them to notice. Many times they would not, and that told me that they were not in control of their funds and they were not as careful with public money as they should be. I had long conversations with other institutions and tried to explain how to treat donors, show gratitude and appreciation. For although we don't want a bottle of Blue, we do want to know that our donation, no matter the magnitude, is appreciated and valued. I was right, but I could not fix the world.

I also couldn't get the balance right between public recognition and anonymous giving. My instinct was always not to be named, but found two main issues with this approach. Firstly, I believe that our children needed to know that we are only custodians of what we have. Secondly, public generosity inspires others to do likewise. But I remained uncomfortable, as I don't believe that being named is ever seen in a good light, and being bathed in that good light was clearly something important to me.

I also firmly believe in social responsibility and have had many discussions with fellow donors. I have often found that they give to causes, not because they believe in the leadership or sometimes even the institution, but because it is simply because it is easier to write a cheque than to say "No". It avoids confrontation and takes less time. But it is irresponsible, because it enables poor management, sustains organisations that shouldn't be sustained and doesn't force introspection of the institution. I believe that this also leads to donor fatigue, as it is not possible for resentment not to build. This will ultimately affect more than just that institution.

Chapter Fifteen

BLUE, BLUE, BLUE, BLUE, ~~BLUE~~, PINK

DURING THIS TIME, our family grew. The banner was blue and then blue and blue and then blue and then, three years after our fourth son Judah was born, Heidi fell pregnant with our fifth child. This time she was aware in advance of the emotional and mental strain of a pregnancy, and managed it accordingly.

The pregnancy was a reasonable one and we eagerly awaited the birth of our fifth son. As Heidi had come from a family of six girls, we had little doubt that we were going to balance nature and that we would only have boys. We simply didn't do girls.

Until Abigail Rose entered our lives. As with the rest of our children, Abby was born by caesarian section, which we planned for a Monday in order to give Heidi enough time to be home for the weekend and for the circumcision, which was now clearly not going to happen. Hillel, her obstetrician and family friend performed the procedure in an atmosphere that was relaxed and jovial. It was, after all, our fifth child and the process did not stress us. And then, after the preparation that accompanies this procedure, he pulled out the baby and shouted "It's a girl! You guys have a girl!" We were completely confused and for once I was at a loss for words.

"Hillel, are you sure?" Heidi asked him, and without missing a beat he answered, "Yip, Heidi, I have done this before you know."

And with that, our lives turned pink. Balloons and dresses and toys filled our home and nine years later continues to do so. Although I always felt very close to my boys, there is for me an intangible and very special bond between a father and daughter. Girls challenge you on levels that the boys don't. They are masterful at a look that says it all, they manipulate and they love with all their hearts, and they are so emotionally smart that it's dangerous. For the first time I felt the vulnerability of my children and the immense need to protect.

I think that children of a "banner holder" have a particularly tough time. But the lowering of it is even tougher for them. They appreciate the importance of appearances and see the advantages it brings to many areas of life. The knowledge and understanding of presentation is critical to function successfully in any environment and picking up on social nuances is an enormous asset. But in my case it was very challenging for them to know where the banner ends and their father began. And when it did come down, what they had to face, each in their own way, is that what was real and what was an image I held for myself, for my family and for those outside my door.

I have been blessed to be able to develop a unique language of communication with each of my children. Having learned from my father that one size does not fit all; I knew that it is the interests and language of the child that needs to be followed in order to establish those skills.

Zac had been born by C-section after a 15 hour unsuccessful labour. He had a cone-shaped head from being stuck in the birth canal, a recessed jaw and puffy eyes. He looked like an alien. He was the most beautiful baby we had ever seen. We had decided that if we had a boy we would call him Aaron Nathan as we liked those names, but looking at him, we knew it was not what he was meant to be called.

Zackary was not a common name at the time and people were a little appalled by it. Heidi's great-grandmother was a sweet and kind lady who told me with real conviction that she thought the name we had chosen, Lasagna, was "lovely".

It should be noted that she never could quite remember my name. I was always referred to as "that nice boy that Heidi married".

Not everyone was so supportive, but that didn't matter to us. With Zac, communication was simple as he spoke the words that I did. Our shared fascination with politics, religion, history and literature made it easy to communicate. He faced the challenge of being our eldest child, which made him the recipient of our pressure and expectations. He became Head Boy without understanding if he was doing this for himself or for us and I suspect that this will be his challenge throughout his life. He will need to understand what his motivations and drivers are and whether he is chasing a goal for the value of it, or rather for the conquest. He is a born leader and will carry that responsibility wherever he goes. He has recently married his soul mate, Zara, who challenges him and connects with him on all levels, and I believe that they will become a formidable couple.

When Ben stopped crying, it became imperative to find a common language for us to speak. What we noticed early on was that he seemed to seek comfort in animals and enjoyed nurturing. This meant that we would endure every phase that this would allow. Dogs, cats and fish quickly progressed to hamsters, lizards and then snakes. These snakes were kept alive by feeding them live rats every Friday and this became part of the family ritual. Neighbours children would pop in to watch the feeding which was creepy and enthralling, and it was a little like having Animal Planet in our home.

I will never forget one horrible Sunday being dragged to a reptile store and to my surprise, actually quite liking a yellow Burmese Python on sale. Ben was smitten and had to have it. I could see the appeal. I took out my credit card to pay when Heidi approached.

"Have you asked how big it gets?" she enquired suspiciously. Of course I hadn't and asked the salesman the question. "Come, I'll show you an adult," he said, and took us to an area where they had built a room for what was the biggest and scariest snake I had ever seen. Apparently they ate rabbits. "Are you serious?" screamed Heidi, no longer breathing steadily. "It could eat one of my children!" she shouted, pointing to Abby who was smiling stupidly, not contemplating the thought of being snake-food. The salesman shook his head in disgust, knowing full well that he had just lost his sale, and explained, "It can't", he said irritably, "It can constrict and maybe kill them, but it won't ever eat them." That not being a real comfort to us, we left the store and went home, Ben sobbing all the way for the loss of his potential new best friend.

Ben has always recoiled from false images and the need to please. Initially he established himself as "the rebel" as he made an active decision not to compete with the seemingly "perfect" older brother. He would be the kid to call us from the school cloakroom at age 11 to quickly give us "my side of the story before the school calls you", when he swore at a teacher (who might well have deserved it) and who would be friendly with the boys who would be asked very nicely to leave the school. He has taken the decision to study psychology, which is an excellent choice for him, given his intuition and insightfulness. He is smart, funny, and one of the kindest and most caring people I know.

One would never have thought so when he was six and Zac was eight. I was at an important lunch at a really beautiful restaurant in Bryanston, North of Johannesburg. We were sitting outside on the terrace and I was doing my best to charm. The purpose of the lunch was to solidify and negotiate an equity interest in a chrome mine that had recently listed in London. Our goal was to purchase a minority interest along with the marketing rights for the chrome that was to be produced, giving us the competitive edge that we were looking for. I was trying to demonstrate what stable and reliable partners we would be, both on the business and the personal side, which was obviously important. Heidi was away so when I received a phone call from home, I knew I had to take it.

It was Zac, and he was panicking. He had locked himself in the bathroom and was convinced that Ben was going to stab him with a Swiss Army knife I had recently bought him in Zurich. He didn't seem to be exaggerating as I could hear Ben screaming from outside the door, something to the effect of, "I am going to kill you! I swear to God I am going to kill you! Open the door so that I can kill you!"

The anger management psychologist that we took him to a few days later helped, and it was advised for him to draw Zac's face on a pillow so that he could punch it whenever the urge to stab him arose. This seemed to help as did confiscating all pocket knives. Of course the lunch ended with a sympathetic nod of understanding from the CEO who had 2.2 children and on his fourth glass of Chardonnay was clearly wondering why it is that we have so many children if they are constantly running around stabbing each other. I have to say, at the time I might have wondered the same thing.

Alex was also a challenge as he embraced and identified and held up the banner of the third and neglected child with conviction. This meant that he relied on his older brothers being the centre of attention, but felt ignored and neglected at the same time. He also didn't own a facial expression until he became a teenager and for years we could not figure out if he had a very dry sense of humour, or simply none at all. But, he was always morally upstanding and had a profound sense of right and wrong. I never recall him telling a lie and he always sought the truth. Unknown to us, however, he was also suffering from petit-mal seizures which made life particularly difficult for him as it meant that there were constant "shorts" in the conscious screenplay which affected many areas of his life.

We thought he might be ADD like the rest of us, and although the psychiatrist wasn't convinced that he was, we tried him on Concerta to see if this would help. What this did achieve was to exacerbate the seizures until they were no longer petit mal. After what I think is a particularly crude process where we had to sleep deprive him, give him as much caffeine as he wanted and let him play computer games for the duration of the night, tests were performed and it was confirmed that he suffered from temporal lobe epilepsy. We now knew what we were dealing with and could treat accordingly. He was 12 when diagnosed and aside from "break through" absent seizures from time to time, has been pretty well under control for some years now.

In a strange way, what this did was give him something that identified him as being unique. And once he was able to feel this, as well as "more normal", thanks to the medication, we were able to establish a relationship with a language that we all enjoy. He has a very high EQ and a sharp mind and once able to let go of the inscription that he wrote at a young age, is free to be who he wants to be.

I was absent during the first few years of Judah, our fourth son's life. I have little recollection of him as a baby and I am pained by this. When I think back on the journey that I have travelled, I have very few regrets as I know that every event has led to another, and that every challenge and difficulty leads and will lead to an opportunity. Yet the one regret that I do have is missing Judah's early years. I know that this was the time when we were aggressively growing the business, but I also know, as trite as it sounds, that this is something I can never get back. I can have an outstanding relationship with him at 12 years old, as I do today and I can relate to him as the person that he is and he will be, but I can never hold him in my arms as a vulnerable, dependent and all-trusting baby ever again. It is a loss that I will live with forever.

Judah sees the world in a unique way. He suffers from a learning disability, which makes him compensate in other areas. His early schooling was a challenge and we could not ascertain whether he was immature or learning disabled. We kept him back in Grade One, in the hope that time was all that was required for him to manage the work load, but this proved to be a waste of time. He is now at a special-needs school and is thriving. He is super smart and doesn't miss a social cue or nuance. We accept that he will never read a book with ease and we rely on dialogue and audiobooks to educate him and increase his vocabulary. He has refined his observation and social skill and can detect a hint of untruth the minute it is uttered. This is of course a curse and a blessing and I am excited to see where his journey takes him, as I know it will not be ordinary.

The choice to lower my banner has presented different challenges for all my children. What interests me is that none of them were affected by my two assaults, as would have been expected. The one attack that took place in our driveway was one that I assumed would have a great impact as we could not delude ourselves that our sophisticated security system and 24 hour security guard was any real protection. But it seemed to have no impact on them. No nightmares for the younger two, no need for trauma counselling for the older ones. For them life simply went on as it had always done.

To my mind this meant that they are very secure or, of the mistaken belief that Dad is all-powerful and can come to no harm. And this is why I believe that my telling them that I am not immortal, not all-powerful and can be vulnerable, and that I have the same fears, anxieties and concerns as perhaps they do, is what is unnerving for them. It was not the attacks that have traumatised, but rather the lowering of the banner.

I have tried to explain that not everything that I held up is untrue, and it's not about turning everything on its head. We are made up of different parts and electing to be only one of those is limiting and ultimately damaging.

It is also difficult for others around me. Heidi has embraced my journey and I am deeply grateful for the space and latitude that she has allowed me. Our relationship, too, has been redefined as, for the first time in our 23-year marriage I cannot, or choose not to, carry the burden of making sure we are all okay. It took a while to reestablish the dance of our marriage, for Heidi to be able to be concerned for my emotional well-being, and more difficult for me to allow it.

For my parents, my siblings, my brothers-in-law, this has not been easy, as I had always displayed a likeable and attractive version of myself, and most importantly I made everyone feel safe. By removing that element, I have left them somewhat adrift and I have created confusion. I am no longer "trouble-free motoring". I am not the poster boy for what "every family needs". I am no longer the fixer, problem-solver and Mr Dependable. Unless, of course, if I choose to be.

Friendships have strengthened and weakened. I now need to receive care as much as give it, and those friendships that allow two-way traffic have become more meaningful and more precious. Those that have not adapted are under strain, and I am not sure whether they will last.

And as I go through this process I am becoming more and more aware of the number of people doing the same. Men and women in business, religious leaders and housewives. Teenagers and children are being schooled this way. My deep concern is that it is not sustainable.

I firmly believe that we need to understand: what are we writing on our banner? How did we come to write it? How does it differ from who we really are? What are we afraid of people seeing when the banner is lowered?

I do not advocate that we lay ourselves bare, willy-nilly, to the world for all to see (despite what I am currently doing). Presentation and marketing and a positive demeanor are vital for survival and success. But as long as we have people in our lives who we can trust to see what lies beneath and as long as we ourselves can be honest enough to know who we are, who we really are, then we can survive our own existence in a positive and successful way.

I know that this is hard for my children to see, no matter how old they are. But I believe that the ability to achieve this is a result of real confidence and positive self-esteem. What I hope for more than anything in the world, is that they can see this journey as positive, take it on board and simply be confident about who they are, how they are powered and what they can achieve by knowing themselves.

Chapter Sixteen

MASTER OF THE UNIVERSE – WORSHIPPING THE MASTER OF THE UNIVERSE

GOD AND I have always had a very real relationship. We spoke all day every day, and although we didn't necessarily agree on all the choices that we both made, we acknowledged and accepted that He was running the world and pretty much does as He chooses.

From a young age, I believed that He had high expectations for me and that I was destined to make a difference. My acceptance of this role meant that what He blessed me with was a part of the plan and that I would have the responsibility to work as hard as I could in order to be the benefactor of such an honour. Secondly, I had a fiduciary responsibility to utilise anything of which I was a custodian, to the best of my ability. There were, of course, some grey areas and I was confident that He would turn a blind eye to some of the extravagances as long as the general agreement was upheld.

It was not always easy for me. The style of religious leadership that I was exposed to in my youth was very different to the approach that seems prevalent today. It was harsh, unforgiving, and in many cases, unkind. Many of our teachers were the products of dysfunctional environments themselves, many grew up without the love required to teach and I was often afraid of their unpredictability. Violent eruptions were common and we were taught in fear. Canings were lashed and wooden blackboard dusters were hurled at our heads. Public humiliation was commonplace. Although other children might not have been affected by this, I was and I became cynical and contrary.

After being publicly beaten in fourth grade, I kept my head down and stayed out of sight until later in high school where I had the confidence to challenge that which I was not comfortable with.

Not that that was well received. Ben made a remark to me a few months ago that he gets annoyed when the kids are told they can ask any question but are viewed as a heretic when they do. This sums up many of my teachers who were often brought out from different countries and transplanted in a place where no one would grow. They taught without joy and I bucked against this, and as a result, didn't achieve.

We often debate religious subjects and notions with our children, all of whom have their own style and approaches. The one aspect that I try and put across to them more than anything, is no matter what one's thoughts are in terms of the Afterlife, of God and creation, or the standard of religious observance, so many aspects of living a disciplined and measured life will bring its own reward. For me it certainly has. I shudder to think what would have been, given my predilections, were it not for these measures and constraints.

So far each of our children, as they have reached 17 or 18 has had a crisis of faith. As scary as this was for us the first time, when Zac went through this, we realised that this is an important part in consolidating and making their faith their own. I don't believe that this is something that every person need go through, but I do believe that it is part of living consciously.

Fortunately, I had grown up in a religiously-observant family. My father took his time in embracing the lifestyle fully (he came from a very traditional and involved family but was not that observant), but my mother was consistent and committed throughout. The result was a healthy, open approach that was coupled with a fundamental belief in not only God, but in a Benevolent and Loving One. I believe that the one common factor amongst all of my siblings (aside from high cholesterol, reflux and diminished height, and maybe the love of coffee), is unwavering faith, and a positive relationship with God. Through the narrative that I received at home, I was able to distinguish between God and his emissaries, many of whom have not been appointed by Him, and between religion and its perversions.

But with success, the foundation of the relationship became unstable. The irony is that there are few industries where you have less control of the major forces that determine success.

Fluctuating metal prices, exchange rates, fuel prices, strikes, off-spec material, derailments, customer and bank liquidity constraints are all some of the factors that keep a trader up at night and most of these are not within his control. And yet, the more successful he is, the more he feels like he is the Master of the Universe.

But when someone bows down to you, or when the custodians of your faith treat you as though you are Divine, when your quips are funnier than others' jokes, and your children are more special than their peers, then it's all too easy to get confused.

I never thought I was God. I never forgot that everything I was blessed with came from Him. But I pushed the boundaries of our faith and its laws.

Keeping strictly-kosher in China was a particular challenge and recalling (another) dinner where my host advised me that the dish I enquired about was vegetarian. I was about to help myself when our China Representative caught my eye and shook his head very slightly, so that no one else would see, in order to communicate that this was not the case. Gerson and I ate peanuts and cabbage that meal. But I have no doubt that many a non-kosher foodstuff passed my lips when I was not being careful enough. When you are hungry and alone it's not difficult to convince yourself of anything.

Shabbat and festivals were enormously challenging, as we are required not to work or use technology. No email, no phone and no contact. Saturdays were generally manageable as the world slowed down but I would not be able to wait for one minute after the day ended in order to see what I had missed. For at least an hour after the end of the day, I would not be able to do anything but work. I often felt that Shabbat saved my life as I was forced to put everything down for 25 hours a week. And as scary as that was, it was a drop of normal in a sea of crazy that kept me, my marriage, and my children alive.

Festivals were even more a challenge as these often would fall on a weekday. I had an arrangement with my staff that if the wheels really did come off, they could drive to my house and I would advise how to handle it. It happened on a few occasions but mostly, to my shock, life went on without me. The stress however would have a massive impact on me and on the enjoyment of those special days. And whereas most people would bask in serenity of the days, and focus on the time with family and friends, I fought raging internal wars with my anxiety, impatience and obsessive thoughts relating to what I was missing, what was potentially going wrong and how I would deal with it afterwards.

But I looked calm and I played my role. It would only be blatantly obvious if you were at our house an hour before the end of the festival. You would witness the stress that had by now, with 60 minutes to go, reached crescendo. It would be hard for me to breathe when the day ended and I would charge upstairs, blinded in panic to pick up my BlackBerry and phone. I would desperately scroll through the hundreds of emails that I had missed, scanning to see if there was an aberration or something that signalled trouble, before sitting down and going through the emails one at a time for the next few hours before I would be able to exhale and breathe again.

I did this for fifteen years.

Chapter Seventeen
UP-TO-SPEED

COMMODITY TRADING IS about information. It is about knowing what price point your competitor is buying at, what his logistics costs are, what product is moving into the international markets, what deals are being spoken about and what new product will be coming on stream. It is also about understanding global trends and events that occur, which might shift a focus or create scarcity or oversupply.

The newspapers arrived daily to the office, the TVs were always on a news channel. Every so often everyone would stop and be drawn to an event of interest, but more so to one that might have an effect on our world.

If you were not up-to-date, you were not up-to-speed, and if you were not up-to-speed, then you were weak.

The result was obvious and predictable. News, both local and international, became an obsession. And the more technology developed and the more Apps that became available, the more you could know and the more that you needed to know. It transcended trading and took on a life of its own. The more a trader knew about an international or local event, the more he controlled the world.

Staff would have to ask permission if they wanted to change the TVs from a news channel to a sports channel. Often this was denied, even for an important game. The repetitive news cycle playing over and over was considered more important, even though there was no real value in it.

Plane accidents were a morbid fascination. As part of the travelling club, even though we all pretended to be above the fear of flying, many were drawn to the Plane Crash Investigations that somehow always seemed to be on the TV late at night when you returned to your hotel room – tired and at risk. Invariably that is when I'd stop flipping channels, although I needed to keep moving, and get drawn into the events that saw a particular flight going down. It was hard not to imagine the feelings of those on the flight and repercussions that followed.

We were careful about Gerson and me travelling on the same flight, but it couldn't always be avoided. I recall one particular harrowing flight from Mauritius to Madagascar, which should have been quick and painless, when I really believed we might not see our destination. But there were countless incidents where we were caught in a storm and the plane struck by lightning (it happened on three occasions), a landing aborted for various reasons, where someone died on a flight, when we missed connections, or simply did not leave. This is part and parcel of a life of travel and although I could tell from the sound of the engines what altitude we were at, or if the flight path into an airport had changed, I eventually learned to relax somewhat and enjoy the short time without connectivity.

Chapter Eighteen

THE PERFECT STORM

WE HAD BRILLIANT years and then we didn't. We lived in a world of numbers that didn't make sense in reality. Our monthly Value Added Tax (VAT) refund was substantial and our volumes were consistently increasing year on year. We dealt in telephone numbers and floated above the norm.

We managed the crisis of 2008 by dealing with each customer and supplier and although we had to rewrite stock values, we did so with elegance and relative ease. We were proud of our handling of the situation and the depths of the relationships that we established.

But the market was slowly changing. Competitors started to take note of what we had achieved, and as a pure trading company we became vulnerable. Realising that we needed security of supply we started to look into upstream projects where we acquired a mine, or a portion of it, along with the marketing rights.

Our first mistake was to approach this with a trader mind-set. Although we were good traders, we were simply not miners. The resource sector requires the patience that most traders don't have. It is also a completely different skill set and we should have built a division with this in mind. We lost around USD5M in Zimbabwe trade and around USD2M in South Africa before we took the painful decision that this was simply not our core focus. It also caused major rifts in the senior management of the business (by now 6 people) and ended with one of them leaving on particularly acrimonious terms. We were a privately held company with no "big daddy" and no deep pockets, and the loss of these funds placed the company under insurmountable strain.

And then there was the market. With headwinds against us, the Chinese battling their own liquidity crises, commodity prices moving steadily down as more production entered the market, production costs moving upwards and margins diminishing, with well-funded competitors buying market share by paying too high a price for material in order to move the volumes, we were slowly heading into the perfect storm. For the first time in our history there were trades we were now losing money on. Margins were tight and any mistake could push a trade into negative territory.

The barometer was dropping, and the sun went behind the clouds. The office became less joyful and the team more stressed. Bonuses were curtailed and resentment started to build. Everyone hunkered down and we faced the oncoming turbulence with rigidity.

This was our next error. As a company we held the banner when we should have lowered it. We were caught up in "who we were" – the biggest in the industry, the strongest force, builders of the market and of course the "kings of chrome". Instead of lowering the banner, reducing staff, not doing business for the sake of market share we stood rigid in the wind and worried about our reputation and not our business. We believed we could sail through it as we had always done.

Gerson saw this ahead of time, but we were not always able to communicate well and, as always, got caught up in the arguments we'd had from our "first year of marriage" instead of making the grown-up decisions we should have done. So, we made some changes – which were hard to do – but it was tokenry. We effectively threw a few sand bags off the vessel and hoped that it was enough. It wasn't.

The banks, our best friends in good times, and the beneficiaries of many years of profitable trade, became nervous. The pressure increased. The wind picked up and we held on tight.

And then I was attacked. And everything became confused.

Chapter Nineteen
LOW IRON

AFTERWARDS, WHEN I stood in my lawyer's office and shakily held a glass of cold water in my hand, I had no idea what was to come. I calmed down, told Heidi I was fine, arranged to get a replacement phone and car key (as they had taken mine) and I managed to pull myself together, before heading back to the office. Sure I was shaken, but "I was fine". I really was.

Until I got sick. It was nothing serious at first, just a cold. I had never, in all my years at work, taken a sick-day. And there was no reason to do so now. But it started to worsen, and I went to a friend who was a physician. He didn't tell me to take bed-rest, as he knew it was a waste of time to even suggest it. And I got worse. He arranged for further tests. I had terrible sinusitis and bronchitis, and I wasn't improving. I became so weak that I battled to get to the end of the driveway. I found walking difficult and the thought of socialising almost unbearable. I had the perfect reason to avoid people as I was ill. I had further blood tests and x-rays and still I deteriorated. I refused to accept that it was linked to my trauma.

My iron was very low and I had to have a gastroscopy and a colonoscopy. Although I was not nervous about having this test, the thought of being out-of-control filled me with dread. On the morning of the procedure the anaesthetist explained that he'd put me to sleep and I wouldn't remember a thing. This wasn't good enough – I needed to understand if I wouldn't remember, or wouldn't be conscious. I could not cope with the thought of knowing that I might have had a conversation but wouldn't remember it. So pathological was my need to "keep it all together".

It was meant to be a joyful time. Zac and Zara were engaged and we planned the wedding for early December. We booked the Johannesburg City Hall, a gorgeous old building with a giant antique organ on the stage. The venue, the food and the event were stunning and we balanced the material with the emotional perfectly. We flew in the band and singers from abroad and it was truly spectacular.

In my speech to the couple I used the theme of "distraction is the enemy" and proceeded to pontificate about the values of focus and commitment. Everyone loved it, as I was a true example of that very idea. Except for one friend who called me aside and said, "You spoke brilliantly but I disagree with everything that you said – distraction is not your enemy, it's exactly what you need." He was also my physician. He knew more than anyone that my intense focus and fixation on keeping the banner in the air was exactly what was doing me harm. If I didn't loosen the death grip with which I was holding on to it, I would be in trouble.

But it was still to get worse.

The wedding was Sunday night. On Tuesday afternoon I was followed home.

As I turned into the driveway and waited for Lancelot, our guard, to open the gate, I saw a new grey Mercedes turn in behind me. I thought nothing of it at first – it is not a conspicuously different vehicle in our neighbourhood. It could have been someone coming to drop a wedding gift or a parent collecting a child from a play-date. It was also 4 pm, an usually early time for me to be at home, so I wasn't used to the flow of traffic in and out of our home at this time.

Suddenly I felt a prickly sensation – something was wrong. The gate opened slowly and I just had enough space to get my car through and put my foot down on the accelerator to get away from who I now knew were my attackers. The flight sensation had kicked in, and I needed to escape. But in doing so, I realised that I would be drawing them closer to the house where Heidi and the kids were. So I braked sharply, threw my hands in the air, to indicate that I was no threat, took a breath and I waited for them to reach me. This act of submission was one of the hardest things I have ever done.

The guy on the passenger side got to me first and pointed his shotgun at me. I tried to open the door, but was now shaking uncontrollably. I managed to open the passenger door by unlocking my door, by which time the second person had reached me. He had been delayed by having to force Lancelot to lie down on the floor and to make sure that he would cause no trouble. They took my watch and wallet and two cellphones, and then my briefcase with everything in it, including my passports. In 45 seconds they were gone.

I was bewildered. I stood next to my car with my hands on my head in complete disbelief. Within three months, it had happened again.

One of the most interesting and frightening aspects of the attack was the debriefing that followed. I was asked to identify the gun that each perpetrator had used. I answered with certainty that the guy on the passenger side was carrying a shotgun, but I couldn't recall the gun that the guy who was right next to me, on my side, was holding – I thought it was a handgun, but couldn't be absolutely sure.

When I said this, I saw the two investigators swop glances knowing that I was not being the model witness, something that was important for me to be. They asked me to think carefully and play the scene out in my mind. And I did. No, I was certain and confident that I had recalled the scene correctly and that the perpetrator further away from me had the shotgun, and the one closer to me had the handgun. This is not something that one forgets.

But I was mistaken, and we had the CCTV tape to prove it. The guy next to me not only held a shotgun, but also kept pushing it in my face. The guy on the far side held a pistol and was much less threatening. My memory had immediately rewritten the event to make it slightly more palatable. I had removed the shotgun from my face and placed it on the far side. I was so confident about this that I would have taken an oath in court to confirm it.

I am told this is the mind's way of coping with a terrible trauma, but in my case, it undermined the very thing that I felt most confident about: my intellect. I had built not only a Tower of Babel with the construct of my world but I had done so with my mind and the power that I believed I had. And in one false memory it all collapsed, and I was left rummaging through the ruins wondering what was real and what was just an illusion.

If I could rewrite history so blatantly and so confidently, how could I be sure of anything?

On the Sunday following the attack, we celebrated my nephew's wedding. I was asked to be a pole-holder, and although I felt a little old for this honour, I was happy to be included. The ceremony was meant to be outside, with beautiful views of Johannesburg, but in typical Johannesburg style, the clouds gathered for a major thunderstorm that afternoon. An alternative venue was quickly sought and found, and everyone moved inside into a hall that was thankfully not being used. Chairs were hastily set out, the flowers moved, and in no time the choir and the musicians were ready to begin.

As everyone settled down, one of the speakers made a sudden sharp sound. Given the circumstances and joviality caused by the storm and the change of venue, this caused no alarm and everyone laughed and continued to enjoy the fracas. Except for me. Although I tried to get into the spirit of the day, the noise had shaken me. I started to feel light-headed as my heart pounded in my chest.

I started sweating and thought that I was going to pass out or throw up. I grabbed Zac, who was near me and told him to hold the pole so that I could leave quickly and get some air. I moved as fast as I could to the room next door and was embraced by the stillness and coolness. I took a deep breath before the dam burst. Before I knew it, I had lost control. I broke down and I sobbed, and I sobbed, and I sobbed. I was inconsolable.

I hadn't shed a tear for my young sister-in-law when she tragically passed away, but the echo of a speaker had brought me quite literally, to my knees.

Heidi had seen me leaving the ceremony and came rushing in to where I had slumped on the floor, in my tuxedo, using the wall for support. She held me in her arms like a child and tried to console me while I wept with abandon. I needed help.

I was suffering from severe post-traumatic stress disorder, but could not distinguish between the stress of my assaults and the stress of the business.

Chapter Twenty

BROKEN BAGGAGE

A FEW MONTHS before this, in order to give the business a better chance of survival, we acceded to some of the banks' pressure and the waters were stilled for a very short period, allowing us to refocus and strategise and for me to enjoy the period leading up to Zac and Zara's wedding.

But it was short-lived. We were clearly only in the eye of the storm where it is momentarily calm. And just as we headed back into the violence that would batter and bruise even the hardiest business, so I was beaten by the assault that would not allow me to stand up.

I called Gerson and told him that I wanted out.

It was not a fair or graceful time to do this. The business was under pressure and we needed all hands on deck. The main problem was that I was not a hand that could be relied on. We discussed the option of my taking a sabbatical and felt that this was the best way not to cause a confidence concern in the business, and also to allow me the time that I needed to regroup and recover.

Fortunately it was December, when the whole of South Africa has the pathological need to shut down. No one cares if there is a storm raging and everyone puts off dealing with anything of importance from around November 15th in case it impacts on their summer vacation. In 15 years Gerson was never able to come to terms with this national quirk, and more so in that year when there was clearly the need to deal with very real concerns.

So I went to Cape Town and stared at the sea and wondered what this was all about. Gerson ploughed through the 400 emails per day and tried to give me my space until he could no longer contain his anxiety. We had never been good at allowing each other downtime, and this was no exception.

So, two weeks into the summer I flew to London to meet him for a day and try and determine a strategy. It was one of the hardest departures I have had. I sat on my bed, I watched violent Atlantic waves hitting the rocks and I used every skill that I was able to access, to put on a brave face, pick up my Tumi carry-on and leave.

I was at the airport and was speaking to Abby, who had just turned eight, on WhatsApp. I had heard a riddle joke, which I asked her, and when she understood it, she burst into a fit of giggles that only a little girl can do. She turned to Heidi who was next to her in the room and said "Daddy is so funny!" Heidi laughed and said, "Yes he is, I sometimes wish I could be so funny." "You can't mom", was Abby's reply, "You have responsibilities!"

That's how good I was.

I arrived in London at 6:30 am. We walked in to the meeting room at 8 am and stayed there until 6 pm. We went for a walk, went back to the airport and flew our respective ways. We had a plan and it was a good one.

Two weeks later the senior management met in Zug, Switzerland, for three days and worked through the six-month strategy. I tried to put on the face of leadership, but I was a shell. I was tired and broken. I was no leader at all.

However, we returned to Johannesburg with purpose and vigour and everyone looked to try and read the situation off every nuance and every gesture. Our team was vulnerable and nervous. Who could blame them?

We retrenched, we explained our strategy to our suppliers, and we got buy-in from the industry. We met with investors who loved our story and our business, and we started to negotiate terms. We didn't hide our position and met repeatedly with the banks to present our options. Their stance was not a flexible one and it was clear that they wanted shareholder investment into the business in order to continue to allow the business to trade.

A trading company might buy and sell commodities but essentially, it turns cash. Without a robust trading facility there can be no business, and we were all too aware of this.

But what they didn't count on was although we would not want to see our dream shattered, and although this was not by any means the way in which anyone wanted to see this concluded, in my case they were pushing someone who had already made a decision to exit the business. I had refused to sign in blood many years before, and I wasn't going to do so now. And for the first time in a while, Gerson and I were on the same page.

We engaged attorneys and worked through the process, trying to get around a table, trying to find a solution, but it was clear it was not going to be resolved. We would have to make the difficult call.

We had a Board meeting and we signed the papers. I was overwhelmed by sadness and by the waste, and also by the quiet way in which it was all happening. T.S. Eliot leapt to mind and I sent a friend a text saying, "That is how the world ends, not with a bang but a whimper." He knew what I was referring to.

For me, a world had indeed ended.

Chapter Twenty One
TOPPLING THE GIANT

AS A CARD-CARRYING member of the banner-holder club, the most challenging aspect was still ahead of me. How was I going to deal with people knowing that my business had failed?

We employed people from our community, I bumped into many of them at the gym, the synagogue, the local coffee bar. I was a public figure of sorts. I had made the choice of holding my banner in the public domain and it was there where I would need to lower it. The very essence of what had driven me to succeed had now caught up with me and I could either choose to face it, or hide from it. This was fight or flight of a different kind.

In a strange way, a few hours after the sadness passed and we told our staff what we had decided, I felt an enormous sense of relief. Although I was not comfortable with how it all ended, I knew that for me that it simply had to. I wanted nothing more than to walk away and to breathe. I knew that I had a hard road ahead, but for the first time in a long while, I felt a budding sense of opportunity and optimism. I was filled with the sense that I was now free to do and become just about anything, aside from maybe an astronaut, or professional cricketer, or plastic surgeon, to name a few.

I was suddenly free to dream.

I also knew that my personal choices would not be viewed by the outside world in its liberating light. No story spreads faster than word that the mighty have fallen.

The very next morning I was sitting in a coffee shop chatting to a friend when a woman I know came up to the table and burst into tears, said very kind things and then holding herself together, turned and left as quickly as she had come. I was speechless. Another person I knew walked in to the same place a few minutes later and mouthed the words, "I'm sorry," across the restaurant, gave me the saddest look known to man and sat down to speak to her friend.

But the phone calls were the hardest. I would never hesitate to call someone if I knew they were going through a difficult time. If I suspected that they would not be comfortable with the call, I would text or email but I had always felt good about doing this. However, being on the receiving end was tougher than I could imagine. Although I was by now pretty much in reasonable shape having dealt with the situation, having felt the sense of relief, having made decisions in terms of taking time off and refocusing my priorities, I found that I was yet again in the role of giving comfort and security even when people were ostensibly calling me to give it.

One call from Mark went as follows, "Hello Howard," in a quiet, sorrowful voice. "Mark!" I said, "What's wrong?" I demanded, not prepared to take on his miserable tone. "Eh, nothing. Are you ok?" he asked, a bit confused by the spring in my voice. "Yes," I said, "But you sound terrible – seriously, anything I can do?" And so it went.

Another was a conversation with my friend Clive. I had called him to tell him of the situation a few days prior and he sent me a text that read as follows, "Howie, just checking that you are ok. I am traumatised by what you told me and I think I need to debrief with you." To which I replied, "Thanks Clive, anytime – happy to be there for you during this difficult time."

My brother-in-law, who runs a very successful company, went into therapy for anxiety, that "if it could happen to you, then it could happen to anyone". My mother kept assuring me that she loved me no matter what happened to the business, which was perplexing, not to mention disturbing. I kept wanting to ask, "Why wouldn't you?" Perhaps I was a little afraid of the answer.

One friend warned me there would be "social fallout" and another one told me that I had dealt people the "Red Ace of Spades" meaning it's a card that no one knows what to do with, and that I needed to allow people to bumble through this as I was doing. It was wise words and I have thought of that analogy often.

But anyone who took the time to engage with me saw that this was a journey that I needed to be on and although difficult was no doubt exactly what God in His wisdom had decided for me and for my family. I have little doubt that good will come of it and I remain a little perplexed by the optimism and sense of adventure that I feel, and am grateful for that, too.

Of course, the industry loves the "Toppling of the Giant", but I have to say that I was genuinely touched by the care and concern of those that we had dealt with for years. Of course there are those who rejoiced in our fall, and that is their prerogative. I have learned that other's reactions reflect more about themselves, their own insecurities, fears, jealousy and emotions than it does much else. I also made a decision not to try and control the dialogue that exists where I cannot see it. A lot that was said would not be true and the futility of engaging and trying to manage it was not something that would serve me. It has been difficult to hear some of it, but I also knew that it would pass.

I am also not prepared to focus only on the last year. It would be ungrateful and irresponsible. What I gained, not only materially from the last 15 years of the business, what my family gained, what we were, and are able to continue to contribute to our family, to our community and to our country cannot be negated. It would be like focusing on the manner in which a person died, rather on the life that they had lived.

There is a prayer that we say on festivals called "Hallel" ("Praise"). It is a collection of six psalms which deal with five fundamental themes of Jewish Faith. What I have always noticed is that in the synagogue when we recite the words, "Give thanks to God for He is good" many people do so by rote and with little real emotion. But when we get to the part where we say "God, save us and bring us success!" voices are raised and we do so with real anguish. I am not a deeply learned person and I have had my own challenges with many aspects of faith, but this has always bothered me. Why is it that we can't thank and appreciate with the same conviction that we beg for salvation? And at a time where we are facing challenges, no matter what they are, I believe so strongly that we have to focus on the immense amount that we have to be grateful for and not on the part that effectively laments our current and fleeting status.

I recall so strongly when Heidi's grandmother was killed, one of the family asked, as one often does in this situation, "Why would God have done this?" and although no one could give an answer, I remember wondering if the same question was asked with regard to all the good that He had bestowed prior to this. I am sure that the answer was no, which did strike me as being a little unfair.

Chapter Twenty Two

WHERE DO YOU GO TO, MY LOVELY?

I HAVE NO idea what my future holds, but nor does anyone else. I am clear that I am in the middle of a healing process, and that it will not be a straight line upward. I am well aware that I might well be putting down one banner in order to raise another. I might very well, in a few years, be holding the very banner I was forced to put down. But I don't think so.

More than anything, my quest is to understand what it was that I needed the world to see, what motivated me to present such a limited and contrived image, and what aspects of what I wrote is true to who I am. For I firmly believe that what I held up was not all a fiction, it was simply a one-dimensional view. But what it did do, was limit me in so many ways that it was actually quite tragic.

As a result of my experience, I can spot other members of this elusive club a mile away. And whereas I am cautious to project my own experience on others, I believe that so many people remain trapped by the fear that if they let people see who they really are, they will be rejected. What they don't realise is that revealing a real person with the confidence to be who they really are, with strengths and weaknesses and vulnerability, is so much more attractive. It is easier for me to spot the businessmen, but I can also see a category of perfect moms, of lofty religious leaders and, of course, cool teenagers, and I am saddened by the price that they are paying to uphold their image.

That said, despite that which I have done by telling my story in its rawest form, I don't believe it is important for everyone to do so, unless the environment is safe. I don't believe that we need to expose our naked and sometimes ugly emotions and drivers, and should not assume that everyone wants or needs to see them. But we do need to understand them, for ourselves at the very least.

I have a friend who is living my life. He holds a senior position in a major international engineering company, travels like a demon. He has a beautiful wife and four wonderful children. He is very active communally, and everyone wants to be him. We threaten meeting for coffee weekly and do so once in a while where we skirt around anything real, until just before it's time to leave. He is partially-present at best and I can read his internal dialogue as we sip cappuccinos. He feels guilty about meeting during office hours (but will only get home at 10 pm), he is worrying about the emails he has not responded to and everything he is letting drop whilst talking to me. He instinctively and anxiously looks at his phone every 35–45 seconds and that reassures him that the world is still turning. Underlying it all is the fear that he is wasting the best years of his life, and that it could be so much better than this.

The saddest thing is that I know that something will give. I have no idea if it will be the death of his cat or the death of his marriage. If it will be a follow-home crime, or loss of his job. If it will be the anxiety that is building in his children, or his health, but the one thing that I have no doubt about, is that the strain of carrying his banner as high as he has chosen to lift it, will not be something that he will manage for much longer.

And although he is drawn to me and recognises that I am living his life a few years ahead, he is paralysed by fear, which has him gripping that banner even tighter. It's a shame really.

I also don't believe that people only write positive messages on their banner. Everyone knows people who are lifetime victims. They rejoice in their status that life is hardest for them, they perpetuate and celebrate misery and are as afraid to acknowledge positivity and optimism, as I have been fearful to recognise the negative.

I will never forget overhearing a conversation that my late grandmother was having with my father. My aunt Jean was meant to take her to the shops (she never learned to drive) in order to look for a dress for a family function. Jean, however, was a severe asthmatic and had to be hospitalised after having a sudden attack. My father told my grandmother the story and she shook her head whilst listening. "It's unbelievable," she said,

"Everything happens to me!".

It dawned on me a few weeks ago when Alex, our third child and my nephew, also a third-born, were chatting. I noticed that their conversation was interlaced with "we are the ignored third child" dialogue. I paid little attention to the conversation and then the next morning was sitting in the room with Alex when Heidi offered him a croissant. He didn't respond, so she offered again, and still he didn't hear. It didn't bother Heidi that she had asked him a third time before he responded. And then it all came together for me.

Had Alex asked Heidi a question three times before getting an answer, this would have "proved" to him that no one takes notice of him, and would have added another thin layer to the proof of what he already believed. Heidi on the other hand, being the eldest, might have other issues, but this was not one of them, and so this interplay had no impact on her. I realised, sitting there, that we choose the events that reinforce the image that we create and validate this on a constant basis.

So I called Alex and my nephew aside later that day when we were together, and explained to them that they could be so free if they let the third-child-thing go, and not feel compelled to only have this as an identity within the family. I know so many adults that hold on to their "stuff" and relish in the unfairness of it all in fear of who they might be if they don't have that to rely on. I am not certain that I had any impact on these 16 and 17-year-olds, but perhaps something will sink in.

Everyone's past has shaped them. Good, less good and bad,

but I believe that understanding what it was in your past that has enabled you and formed you, accepting the responsibility that the rest of your life is yours, is key to being comfortable to present a less contrived and multi-faceted individual.

I also know that perspective is fleeting. The ability to be honest with ourselves is limited, something that we are not always able to do. There are times when we need to move the "shotgun" further from our face. But then, when we are safe, we need to acknowledge the choices we made and to understand why.

In putting together this work, I asked my siblings if the perspective that I have of my life and my childhood is one with which they agree. My older brother felt that I portrayed a one-dimensional and limited perspective of myself – I was never "The Wolf of Wall Street". I was both relieved and a little offended by that, although it was clearly meant as a compliment. He felt that I was more connected to my children than many other men. Although I might have become this over the last few years, this was never who I was and who I am today.

He felt that the portrayal of my childhood was pretty accurate, and that I had even minimised some of the more bizarre aspects that we grew up with, given the eccentric nature of our parents. How could I have not mentioned the weekends away with the family? He also reminded me of the times, as children, that we would go to Swaziland for weekends.

Gambling was not legal in South Africa but my parents enjoyed this pastime, and so we would pack the Hi-Ace and drive five or six hours, depending on the queues at passport control, and stay at the Ezulwini Holiday Inn near Mbabane. We would have a great time during the day, swimming and marauding, and then would spend the nights riding the shuttle bus that moved guests between the Ezulwini at the bottom of the hill and the Royal Swazi Spa at the top where the casino was situated. Up to the top and back again, and again, and again.

One Saturday afternoon when I was around ten, we were playing in the kids playground where there was a very impressive wooden structure.

My uncle had joined us for the weekend. He was wild and a little out of control, which meant that we were immediately drawn to him and would follow him anywhere. He convinced us to hang on our hands from a bridge and "walk" across, moving slowly from one side of the bridge to the other. I was very nervous to do this, but he convinced me that I could manage, promising me that he would catch me if I fell.

Well I did and he didn't. I fell badly. It was clear that I had broken my arm (the protruding bone being an obvious indication to my ten-year-old brain) and I wondered what would happen next. What did happen surprised me and I will never quite understand the events that followed. My uncle and parents gathered around me and asked me if I was able to move my fingers. I need to add that none of the assembled group had medical training. I tried and I could, and everyone breathed a collective sigh of relief. It was not broken. With such a simple test, I recall wondering, why do we need x-rays at all?

Someone suggested taking me to a doctor, but the idea never

really gathered support, primarily because my mother was horrified by the thought of going to a Swazi Hospital. So we didn't. That night they went to the Royal Swazi Spa to gamble, and I tried to sleep. There were speed-bumps on the hill that led to the Casino and I knew that I would be in too much pain to contemplate negotiating them in the shuttle.

I lay in the dark with my arm raised on a pillow as this seemed to be the most comfortable position, and suffered through the pain. The next morning, after breakfast, (and my father's game of tennis), we packed the Hi-Ace and headed home to Johannesburg. This was 35 years ago and I can still feel each bump and movement along the way. No amount of tape playing Peter Sarstedt singing "Where Do You Go to My Lovely" could transport me away from the excruciating pain that engulfed me.

I didn't go for x-rays that night either.

On Monday morning, (when the stars aligned), I recall going to Rosebank Clinic in Johannesburg to have x-rays, being told that I had not only broken, but severely dislocated my wrist (hence the pain), so only then would my treatment begin. Today I would have been in therapy for months in order to deal with the trauma of the whole event and the neglect of my parents. But then, no one dealt with these things. They slapped on a cast, everyone had a good laugh about it, and my wrist at least, healed.

How did I forget this story? The answer is simple. I didn't, but for me it was an event in my childhood that did not evoke any different feelings or establish a conclusion different to that which I already "knew". It is Alex and the croissant. It is each of our stories that add layer upon layer to that which we have already concluded.

And it is those layers that are so hard to peel away.

Our past has "hardwired" us to react in a specific way to events and to external stimuli. As with everything, these reactions most likely have positive and negative components. Some will assist us and some will limit us. We also need to accept that our childhoods are very much our own perceptions. It is only as a parent that it becomes clear how Heidi and I are the same parents in the same marriage, our children have very different strengths, weaknesses, triggers and feel very differently (in some areas) about our parenting.

I also have no doubt that each child of ours will be able to tell "parenting stories" about us and I am sure that each will be different, depending on their triggers and make up. And whereas some will be their own perception, many will hurt us for the injustice that they feel, as no doubt do my own parents.

Chapter Twenty Three

LUGGAGE FOR CARRYING ON

WE KNOW THAT nothing in life is a constant. Relationships, financial matters, trends, our connection with God, all ebb and flow like the coming and going of the tide. There are times when we have no need to walk towards the sea as it comes to greet us, and there are times when tremendous effort is required just to feel the water beneath our feet.

This work was been captured at a singular moment in my life, a snapshot of time as it were, where the tide hovers in a strange place. In many respects, the water has receded and is far out in the distance, but in others it gushes towards me, and I am embraced by the warmth of its current.

I have emptied my carry-on of items that have weighed me down and I am focused on making sure I have the essentials secured before adding the nice-to-haves. I am blessed to have been able to unpack it all at this stage in my life, and start refilling it piece by piece – gently wrapping and placing the precious requirements in first, so that they are not left behind.

I am 45. I have been married for 23 years. I have five wonderful children and a daughter-in-law. My parents are mostly healthy and live around the corner from us. I have three siblings and their families who live in walking distance and Heidi has four sisters and their families who are also close by. I have a good relationship with my parents-in-law and all my brothers- and sisters-in-law. Some, of course, are better than others, but even if they are imperfect, they need to come along.

I have friends I can talk to and count on for anything and who are friends, not because of what I wrote on my banner, but because of what is behind it. For me, they are important to pack in, too.

I have insight into situations that most do not and appreciate my ability to process matters at the speed and with the clarity that I do. I find myself funny, sometimes really funny, and enjoy my own wit. I am no cricket player and I suck at boxing. But I love it.

I enjoy people. Especially smart ones.

I am no superman, and knowing that lightens my load.

I can be vulnerable.

I am very proud of what I have achieved and of who I am, but I remain disappointed by some of the choices I have made and by my behaviour at times. I have been unrelenting and rigid, judgemental and harsh, when sometimes it has not been the right approach.

Heidi and the children have paid a price. But they have also gained and prospered. And so has everyone around me.

These are my truths and this is my baggage.

I carry with me my daily struggle, which is to know what I can control and what I cannot. It is to accept what I can fix and what I cannot, to know when to engage and when to stay clear. It is also the struggle of being fully focused on what is at hand, and when to allow myself the luxury of being everywhere at once. This is a challenge I will take with me, for now.

It is the struggle of letting go, exhaling and trusting that if I do my part, then God will do His. It is the challenge of knowing that I am not able to run the world, I can just assist in making it a better place to be. It is the acceptance that I don't only have value when I overachieve, that I don't need to be Superman to have value.

My gifts are numerous, my limitations many. I am kind and unkind, real and fake. I am giving and I am selfish. I am what I choose to be.

And with my banner lowered and my carry-on packed, I can indeed be anything (except for a cricketer and Superman). And I will probably never be good at boxing.

ACKNOWLEDGEMENTS

THE WRITING OF this book has not been easy for those around me.

In many ways, it has been a selfish journey that has challenged and altered perceptions, dealt with issues that are more comfortable left undisturbed, and generally upset just about everyone.

My parents, in particular, have suffered through not only dealing with having a slightly "eccentric" son, but also having to deal with being painted in a light that reflects only my reality. And in many cases it is a "reality" as seen through the eyes of a child. What I do acknowledge, is that no matter how painful it must be for them to read these perceptions, they have allowed me to write, and even given me their support, through this process. Ironically, the hours of discussions around so much of our history has given me an adult insight into their world, and that like anything else worthwhile – brilliant and hard and wonderful and challenging. Despite all that I have written, I could only do so because I was brought up in their home, a place where I was taught to think and to challenge and to love and to fight, but to do it all with passion. For that, and so much more, I thank you.

Heidi, who has lived with, and tolerated, my obsessiveness, is indeed my "drop of normal in a sea of chaos". She allows me space to be who I need to be, and has supported and loved me through it all. She is my Ithaca that I can return to when the monsters get too scary. She is my rock and my island, and I know that whatever my journey, she is there to guide me and keep me safe. Our relationship is a gift from God – I am so grateful.

My children, Zac and Zara, Ben, Alex, Judah and Abigail – each of you has engaged and challenged me, loved me and supported me. Tolerated my "putting down the banner" even when having dad do so must be scary. You have accepted that I need to travel this journey, and I thank you for readily packing your bags and coming along. I am so blessed by the relationships that I have with each of you. Each is real and different and special. To Abby, who at nine has read every word and every iteration of the text, debated and commented on every nuance: I know I dedicated this book to mom, but you know it's really for you (just don't say anything).

My siblings Adi, Sean and Alon: it cannot be easy to have our childhood made public property, and I hope that it does not cause discomfort. Adi, you lit the spark of literature in me as a young child. Look what you have done! Sean, you are wise and dependable, and a solid constant. Thank you for always being my big brother. Alon, I know that aspects of this book are painful for you, considering the winter period that you have lived through, but I feel so grateful that with Kim in your life, the sun can once again shine. You are a remarkable man.

My in-laws – Selwyn and Joan: thank you for entrusting me with your precious daughter, thank you for introducing me to the world of mining and thank you most of all, for running low on potatoes.

My friends who have watched and guided me, stood by me and supported me, read and reread this manuscript, told me what was crap and what they enjoyed, and who have loved me for me and not for what is on my banner. Thank you.

My business partner and friend Gerson (I will never be able to say 'ex' partner), thank you for putting up with me, for allowing details of this story to be told, and most of all, for the relationship that we have.

My editor Batya Bricker – your encouragement and support and unrelenting attention to detail has made this possible. Please God, this is the first of many.

And to God, with whom I spoke throughout this process, and who was not always happy with me: thank you for Your patience and for giving me the guidance that is taking me where I need to go.

Howard Feldman
7th August, 2014